Ro

S0-ACJ-031

S.148

MEN OF ACTION IN THE BOOK OF ACTS

Books by Paul S. Rees

CHRISTIAN: COMMIT YOURSELF!

THE ADEQUATE MAN

TRIUMPHANT IN TROUBLE

MEN OF ACTION IN THE BOOK OF ACTS

Men of Action

in the

Book of Acts

PAUL S. REES

FLEMING H. REVELL COMPANY
WESTWOOD, NEW JERSEY

Scripture quotations in this publication are from the *Revised Standard Version of the Bible*, copyrighted 1946 and 1952.

COPYRIGHT © 1966 BY FLEMING H. REVELL COMPANY • ALL RIGHTS RESERVED • WESTWOOD, NEW JERSEY • LIBRARY OF CONGRESS CATALOG CARD NUMBER: 66-21903 • PRINTED IN THE UNITED STATES OF AMERICA • 1.1

To
an ageless octogenarian,
A. Lindsay Glegg, Esq.—
graceful as a golfer,
gifted as an evangelist,
gracious as a host,
glowing as a Christian—
my friend

Preface

These biographical sketches, based on the fifth book of the New Testament, are here reproduced mainly in the form in which they were originally given as spoken addresses. This will account for their intimacy and directness of style.

I must acknowledge gratefully the insistent encouragement toward publication of these studies that has come from my esteemed friend, Mr. Wilbur Davies. He and his staff have done everything possible to lighten the load of an author currently engaged in almost constant travel.

"From the lives of men whose passage is marked by a trace of durable light," wrote Louis Pasteur, "let us piously gather up every word, every incident likely to make known the incentives of their great souls, for the education of posterity."

I have but small confidence that I have treated them worthily or well, but my confidence is boundless that the "men of action" whose names follow have left upon the canvas of history more than a "trace of durable light."

Monrovia, California   PAUL S. REES

Contents

Contents

MEN OF ACTION IN THE BOOK OF ACTS

1 Peter:

The Man Who Conquered Fear

TEXT: ". . . when he (Peter) saw the wind, he was afraid. . . ." MATTHEW 14:30.
"Now when they saw the boldness of Peter . . ." ACTS 4:13.

IN THIS SERIES of Bible Studies we shall be thinking about some of the characters that stand out prominently in this remarkable book called the *Acts of the Apostles*—God's Actors in the Book of Acts. You will have noticed that the "Acts of the *Apostles*" is the formal title of the book: God does work through humans. We must never forget that.

It is, however, worth reminding ourselves at the very beginning of these studies that, in point of fact, the *divine* Actor in the Acts is none other than the Risen Christ through His Holy Spirit. The book opens, as you will recall, with an introductory word which Luke the human author, gives to his friend, Theophilus, in which

1

he says, as we have it in the Revised Standard Version, "In the first book"—that is in the Gospel by Luke— "I have dealt with all that Jesus began to do and teach. ...." Ah then, our Saviour had not *finished* when He ascended on high in His glorified form! He carries on through His Holy Spirit, moving upon, ministering within, the redeemed, believing persons who constitute the church that bears His name. Among these is Peter, the man whom Lloyd Douglas calls "The Big Fisherman," who dominates the first part of the Book of Acts just as St. Paul dominates the second part of it.

Peter, of course, offers us a study in many different phases of Christian truth and teaching, of which I have singled out one. I want us to think of Peter from the point of view of the fears that now and again beset him, and how he was recovered and released from those fears, and, by the power of the Holy Spirit, was enabled, as we see him in the Acts of the Apostles, to leave with us an example of magnificent Christian courage.

We need to have something said to us that is helpful and constructive about the subject of fear, because fear in one way or another is a powerful factor in the lives of all of us. In fact, in our generation it plays an almost incredible part in personal life, family life, business life, political life, international life. I suppose it is not exaggerating to say that more books have been written, and more lectures have been delivered, and probably more sermons preached, on the theme of fear in our generation than in any generation that has gone before. I go to libraries, and I find long shelves of books in the psychology and psychiatry division, in which the subject of fear bulks big.

This leads us to remind ourselves, again by way of introduction, that not all fear is bad, not all fear is injurious, not all fear is something from which we would be set free. There are fears that are wholesome. God implanted them. There is, for example, the instinctive fear of danger, particularly some startling physical danger. You are walking down a path and a snake suddenly appears before your eyes, poised and ready to strike. Instinctively you recoil. You may be filled with the Holy Spirit and yet recoil. The fact that you are filled with the Holy Spirit has not destroyed this instinctive apparatus that had to do with fear, because this is part of our God-given emotional mechanism by which physical life is sustained. It is the instinct of self-preservation, in which of course fears plays a part, that leads you to look both ways before you cross a busy road. Someone has said that our modern cities are cities of the quick and the dead, and if you aren't quick you are dead: that's all there is to it! It would be stupid to say, "You know me—I'm filled with the Holy Spirit. I don't need to worry about these things"—and plunge right out into the traffic. Nonsense! Here *God-given* fear generates caution.

On the other hand there are fears that are unwholesome. There are even legitimate fears that, carried too far, become neurotic and obsessive and compulsive. We may develop all sorts of phobias, which in their most acute forms require some special treatment, medical or psychiatric. A mild phobia is not necessarily injurious. Whether mild or acute, phobias tend to be temperamental—i.e., they are peculiar to certain persons. They don't necessarily prey on wide ranges of people. They

3

are characteristic of certain individuals. For example, we have *claustrophobia*. This is the emotional affliction of a person who panics if he is in a place that confines him —a narrow corridor, closely-constricting walls. Mrs. Rees has a touch of what they call *acrophobia*. It is a fear of heights. She doesn't want to sit next to the window in an airplane when we are traveling. It bothers her to look down; it doesn't disturb me one bit. These are temperamental things, having to do with individuals. They are not universal fears.

Then there are fears that relate to character, and to the moral conduct of life. An example would be the fear of criticism, or ostracism, or financial loss, that prevents a man from taking the position in business or politics that an informed and sensitive Christian conscience requires him to take. It is not altogether unusual to find in the life of an obviously genuine Christian a single area of moral cowardice. I think now of one such Christian, a dear man with whom I once prayed nearly the night through, till God mightily met him in the fulness of the Holy Spirit and set him free. He had the courage of his Christian principles and convictions *except in one set of circumstances*. Although he was a man of modest means, he had some rich relatives. They were not Christians. They would occasionally visit him and his family for a weekend. On such occasions they would engage in activities on the Lord's Day that were contrary both to his scruples and to his normal practice. Moreover, by coaxing and wheedling and subtly intimidating, they located the weak joint in his moral armor, and they would succeed in getting him involved in their own disregard for the Lord's Day. But in the night to which

4

I have referred he faced up to the whole thing. This one plague-spot of cowardice was handed over to the lordship of Christ. The control of the Holy Spirit became the all-inclusive thing that Christ wants it to be. He was released—as the after-events demonstrated.

I

THE FAILURE OF COURAGE

Let us turn now to the Gospel by Matthew, the 14th chapter. In this chapter we have the record of that night when our Lord was separated from His associates, His apostled men, for a little while. He was praying, somewhere on the shore, and they were out on the Sea of Galilee in their little craft, being tossed about in a storm. We read in verse 25: "And in the fourth watch of the night he came to them, walking on the sea. But when the disciples saw him walking on the sea, they were terrified, saying, 'It is a ghost!' And they cried out for fear. But immediately Jesus spoke to them, saying, 'Take heart, it is I; have no fear.' And Peter"—now see how Peter moves into the center of the picture—"And Peter answered him, 'Lord, if it is you, bid me to come to you on the water.' He said, 'Come.' So Peter got out of the boat and walked on the water and came to Jesus; but when he saw the wind, he was afraid, and beginning to sink he cried out, 'Lord, save me.' Jesus immediately reached out his hand and caught him, saying to him, 'O man of little faith, why did you doubt?' " And doubting gave way to fear.

Call this *the fear of sinking.* He started all right. He

had his word from the Master, "Come." He went out, *on the water,* on the strength of our Lord's authority and word. But then, getting his eyes off Jesus and on these threatening surroundings, he began to sink and was filled with panic. Young friends, or perhaps I should say young Christians whatever your physical age may be, here is something that should be instructive to all of you: after you have made a beginning, Satan will do his best to frighten you with the thought, "Oh yes, it's all very well to start like this, but you will never be able to hold out! You will not be able to make a go of this thing in a permanent way." The fear of sinking! How often it brings panic and paralysis, maybe utter defeat and discouragement, into the lives of those who have made a beginning with Jesus Christ!

Come to a second instance of the failure of courage in Peter's life. You don't have to go far for it; just turn a page or two here in the Gospel by Matthew, to chapter 16. In this chapter we have the account of our Lord's interview with the apostles far up the north country at Caesarea Philippi. He asked them first about the view of Himself that other men had. "What do they think of me? What do they say of me?" asks Jesus. And they reported to Him: ". . . Some say John the Baptist, others say Elijah, and others Jeremiah or one of the prophets."

Then, you remember, Jesus turns the question on these apostles: ". . . *But who do you say that I am?*" The spokesman is Peter. Simon Peter replied: ". . . *You are the Christ, the Son of the living God.*" A magnificent answer! Utterly correct, superbly right. Then Jesus pronounces a blessing on him because of that confession of faith in His diety. Now, on to verse 21: "From that time Jesus began to show his disciples that he must go to Jerusalem and suffer"—suffer "many things from the elders and chief priests and scribes, and be killed, and on the third day be raised. And Peter"—the same Peter who a moment ago had exhibited such fine insight, such a splendid spirit—"took him and began to rebuke him, saying, 'God forbid, Lord! This shall never happen to you.' But he turned and said to Peter, 'Get behind me, Satan! You are a hindrance to me. . . .'"

Mind you, those words were addressed to Peter by Jesus, when only a moment before Jesus had said, ". . . Blessed art thou, Simon Bar-Jona! . . ." (that is, Son of Jona). Now He says, ". . . You are a hindrance to me; for you are not on the side of God, but of men."

For a clue to this failure of courage on Peter's part note what follows: "Then Jesus told his disciples, 'If any man would come after me, let him deny himself and take up his cross and follow me". Call this *the fear of suffering*. When Jesus disclosed to Peter that He, the Lord, must go to Jerusalem and suffer and die, Peter could not tolerate it. Whereupon Jesus turns to Peter and says, in effect, "Why, Peter, if you are afraid of pain, and especially the pain of self-denial, you will never go far in Christian discipleship."

How this truth needs to be stressed! Perhaps if you will examine failures that have occurred in your own life —failures in the realm of courage—you will discover that those breakdowns have been of this character: you have been afraid of the pain, the reproach, the cost of real discipleship. Dietrich Bonhoeffer, that brilliant young German theologian, who was executed by the Nazis, left

a book, now available in English under the title of
The Cost of Discipleship. In it is a chapter called
"Costly Grace," which is worth twice the price of the
book. Writing as a Lutheran, Bonhoeffer takes the position that multitudes of Lutherans, and other Christians
as well, misunderstand and misuse Luther's teaching on
the doctrine of justification by faith. The abuse consists
in treating the doctrine as if it offered the justification
of *sin* instead of the justification of the *sinner.* So we
are indulgent with ourselves. We are tolerant of sin. We
wage no real battle against temptation. And we com-
placently assume that God will justify all this simply
because we are "believers." "This," says Bonhoeffer, "is
cheap grace." Here is an emphasis sorely needed.
Though we shrink from the cross repeatedly, some of
us almost chronically, still no blush of shame comes
over us.

A few years ago Paul Mallon wrote a book called *The
Ease Era.* The phrase fits our age. Everybody wants it
easy. Self-denial, never easy, is in our day a prime chal-
lenge. We don't like self denial: we are afraid of it. It
is too uncomfortable. Of course self-discipline can be
painful. It is the pain of saying "no" to yourself in this,
or that, or the other, in order that you say a great "yes"
to the perfect lordship of Jesus. This is restrictive. We
rebel against it because it seems to limit our freedom.
This is precisely the point at which many young people
go off the rails. They think falsely about freedom, as
though it were the same as license. I believe it was
G. K. Chesterton who said, "This age insists on being
untrammelled and succeeds only in being unbuttoned."
It was a typically Chestertonian observation—combining

8

the shrewd with the startling. What a sorry spectacle we present to the world, and present to Christ—which is more serious and more to the point—when we will not practice those disciplines and denials which have always belonged to real Christian discipleship!

Augustine, converted to Christ from a life of complete license and licentiousness, was walking along one day when, across the road, coming in the other direction, appeared one of the many mistresses he had known. She didn't know about his conversion. Beguilingly she called to him, "Augustine." He went right on his way. She called again, "Augustine. It is I!" Augustine, scarcely turning his face, said, "Yes, but it is not I!" What if fear had overcome that Christian impulse to deny himself? ". . . let him deny himself and take up his cross and follow me." Let's be clear on it: if you are afraid of the pain of self-denial, your discipleship will be a crippled, useless thing.

Take another instance. This brings us to the failure in Peter's life for which, sadly enough, he is best known. We shall take the account of it in the Gospel by Mark, the 14th chapter. Look at verse 66. "And as Peter was below in the courtyard, one of the maids of the high priest came; and seeing Peter warming himself, she looked at him, and said, 'You also were with the Nazarene, Jesus.'" Do you get the sneering accents of that charge? "But he denied it, saying, 'I neither know nor understand what you mean.'"

The fear of sinking! The fear of suffering! And now *the fear of sneering*. Ask an armed forces man and he will tell you that many a fellow who has the sheer physical bravery to face shot and shell does *not* have the

9

moral courage to stand up to a sneer. Let one of his buddies ridicule him and he wilts. The fear of the sneer! Peter found it deadly, as many of us have.

II

THE FULNESS OF COURAGE

Now! This is the dark side of the picture—the failure in courage—from which we turn to something gleamingly brighter. To those who had known the fickle, faint-hearted Peter it must have been astounding to see him transformed into a man full of courage. I use the word fulness because, whatever it was that happened to Peter and to his fellow-disciples in the city of Jerusalem on the Day of Pentecost, it is described for us precisely in this way. For example, the thrilling second chapter of Acts begins: "When the day of Pentecost had come, they were all together in one place. And suddenly a sound came from heaven like the rush of a mighty wind, and it filled all the house where they were sitting. And there appeared to them tongues as of fire, distributed and resting on each one of them. And they were all filled with the Holy Spirit and began to speak in other tongues, as the Spirit gave them utterance" (vv. 1-4).

This phrase, "filled with the Spirit," stands in grave peril amongst us. It is the peril of the familiar. It is the peril of anything that becomes mere patter. Would God we could rescue it from the threadbare thing that it is in many circles to the thrilling thing it ought to be.

Is there, we may ask, any real connection between being filled with the Spirit of God and the overcoming of fear? If so, what is it?

To the first question we should give a resounding "yes." We should then tackle the second question by saying two things: (1) that being filled with the Spirit means to be possessed by another, whose resources are immeasurably greater than ours; and (2) that, conversely, being filled with the Spirit means to be dispossessed of ourselves, with all those liabilities that our egos carry about with them. That is the answer to the fear problem. In one of those razor-sharp insights that one learns to expect from him, Oswald Chambers says, "Jesus Christ does not deal with my morality or immorality, but with 'my right to myself.'" In any authentic Pentecostal experience this really is what takes place: one consents to the searing flame in which that "right" is consumed.

Think of the failures of courage we have had in *our* lives. Is is not true that each time we have met a defeat it has been because there was too much of ourselves there? When the pressure is on and high decisions have to be made, it is a controlling concern for our own convenience, or comfort, or reputation, or advancement, that gives fear its innings in our lives. But suppose you have got yourself off your hands, have given up your right to yourself, and the Holy Spirit has a managerial grip on you, what in fact is there to fear?

> O fear the Lord, ye saints, and you will then
> Have nothing else to fear;
> Make you His service your delight—
> He'll make your needs His care.

Peter found it so. In the 4th chapter of Acts we learn that it was a "Peter, filled with the Holy Spirit," who

11

said, ". . . Rulers of the people and elders . . . be it
known to you all, and to all the people of Israel, that by
the name of Jesus Christ of Nazareth, whom you crucified, whom God raised from the dead, by him this man
is standing before you well" (vv. 8-10). What was the
effect? Verse 13 reports it: "they saw the *boldness* of
Peter."

III

THE FACETS OF COURAGE

As many-sided as a diamond—each facet a flash of
splendor when held to the sun—was the courage we see
in Peter as his career in the Spirit unfolds.

There was the courage *to take a stand*. In Acts 2:14
we read, "But Peter, standing with the eleven, lifted up
his voice." What that voice gave forth was a brave and
telling witness for the crucified and risen Jesus. Was
this the man who refused to stand up and be counted
when, only a few weeks ago, he was called a follower
of Jesus by a serving maid in the high priest's palace?
Yes, the same man. And yet not the same! The fiery
purging had made him different.

Wendell Phillips was a courageous and eloquent
spokesman for abolition in a day when human slavery
was still practiced in the United States. For his forth-
right stand he was at times bitterly assailed. If his wife
found him wavering, she would say, "Wendell, don't
shilly-shally!" The Holy Spirit had taken the "shilly-
shally" out of Peter's character.

Or take the courage *to speak the truth*. There's a glint

of this facet when, in the story of the arrest of Peter and John in Acts 4, we read their reply to the authorities who would seal their lips, ". . . Whether it is right in the sight of God to listen to you rather than to God, you must judge; for we cannot but speak of what we have seen and heard" (vv. 19-20). I know there are times when "silence is golden." I know also that there are times when silence is craven. Communist inquisitors, trying to force a confession from a Christian bishop, finally resorted to the ghastly "water treatment." The strangling man of God had only breath left to declare, "I serve a Christ who told no lie and He will not allow me to tell one!" The fact that he lived to tell the story does not alter the greater fact that he held truth too dear a treasure to let it go. In a day when truth often goes begging for standard-bearers who will never let it trail in the dust, *that* sort of courage is much too seldom found.

Or think of the courage *to use what you have*. This too we see in Peter. To the beggar at the Beautiful Gate Peter said, ". . . I have no silver and gold, but I give you what I have; in the name of Jesus Christ of Nazareth, walk" (Acts 3:6). You don't have a corps of engineers to get you across the Red Sea: use your rod. You have neither a vast army nor a Maginot Line to defend yourself against the Midianites: use your pitchers and torches. You don't have a king's armor with which to meet Goliath: use your shepherd's sling. You don't have a field commissary with which to feed five thousand: use the lad's loaves and fishes. It takes some brave doing, but get on with it! ". . . I give you what I have. . . ."

13

Or consider the courage *to brand wrong for what it is*. The face of valor is not always gay. Sometimes it is grave. There was a holy sternness in Peter's face and voice when, tearing the mask from a fictitious consecration, he said, ". . . Ananias, why has Satan filled your heart to lie to the Holy Spirit. . .?" (Acts 5:3). There are times when the mincing of words works nothing but mischief. Evil needs to be branded as evil. One of our Congressmen, caught wobbling and welshing on a moral issue that came up for a vote, was reprimanded by one of his constituents. His lame defense was, "But you don't know the outside pressures that were on us."

"Outside pressures," retorted the indignant man, "outside pressures? Where were your *inside braces?*" Precisely! The Holy Ghost had fitted Peter with some inside braces that fortified him for uncompromising dealing with the ugly head of sin when it reared itself.

Or think of the courage *to put the will of God first*. Peter put God's will above *persecution*. The authorities in Jerusalem had laid a ban on the Christian testimony of Peter and his colleagues. When the ban was ignored, they were arrested. Their fearless defense was, as Peter laid it down, ". . . We must obey God rather than men" (Acts 5:29). Moreover, Peter put the will of God above *prejudice*. God had a ministry for him to exercise among Gentiles. Spirit-filled man though he was, there was an honest racial prejudice that stood in his way. A vision from God shook him. Then a call to preach to Gentiles reached him. At which point, says Peter, ". . . the Spirit told me to go with them, making no distinction" (Acts 11:12). And he adds, a moment later, ". . . who was I that I could withstand God?" (v. 17). It was in the true

14

Petrine spirit that, centuries later, one of God's brave and bonny fighters took for his motto: "God's will— nothing more, nothing less, nothing else!"

Or, finally, take the courage *to face the end without flinching*. Anyone who has ever read a book like Oscar Cullman's *Peter* will know how painstaking have been the attempts of New Testament scholars to weigh the evidence of Scripture and tradition with respect to the death of Peter. The amount of research that has gone into the question is all but incredible. Did Peter die in Rome? What was the form of his martyrdom? Was he crucified? If so, was he crucified with head suspended, as one tradition has it? Professor Cullman's conclusion is that the "head downward" rumor has only slight historical support, but that a stronger fabric of evidence upholds the view of his having met death in Rome. The one thing that is clear is the prophetic testimony of John 21:18, 19, setting forth his death in martyrdom.

So, unable to point to any record of the particulars of Peter's death, what more appropriate thing can we do than turn to his own writings and thus be reminded of the radiant hope with which he and his comrades faced death and destiny. "Blessed be the God and Father of our Lord Jesus Christ!" he exclaims. "By his great mercy we have been born anew to a living hope through the resurrection of Jesus Christ from the dead, and to an inheritance which is imperishable, undefiled, and unfading, kept in heaven for you, who by God's power are guarded through faith for a salvation ready to be revealed in the last time" (I Peter 1:3-5).

Perhaps it was a crucifixion to which he was sentenced. While agony succeeded agony, the pain was soothed and the grimness was lit by the glory of a hope that sprang from that sepulcher that Peter had one day found—empty!

The lips are barely moving now. . . .

"A living hope. . . ."

"An inheritance. . . ."

"Imperishable. . . ."

"Undefiled. . . ."

"Unfading. . . ."

"In heaven!"

Only the Master that Jesus is could begin with Peter the Fearful and end with Peter the Fearless!

2 Stephen:

The Man Who Lived at Floodtide

TEXT: ". . . full of the Spirit and of wisdom . . . a man full of faith . . . Stephen, full of grace and power. . ." Acts 6:3, 5, 8.

HAVING LOOKED AT the man who conquered fear, we turn now to a man who lived where the tide of God's Spirit was flowing full. His story begins in Acts 6: "Now in these days when the disciples were increasing in number, the Hellenists murmured against the Hebrews because their widows were neglected in the daily distribution." In the Authorized Version we read "Greeks." These were not Greeks at all: they were Hebrews who, born outside Jerusalem and Palestine, could not claim Aramaic as their native tongue. Their vernacular was Greek, which was the universal language of that day. Hence they are called "Hellenists." Together with the Aramaic-speaking believers they formed the Christian church in Jerusalem.

The complaint that now arose was that somehow, in the distribution of alms that had been collected, the widows of those members of the church who had been born outside Palestine did not receive quite as considerate or generous treatment as the widows of those who were native to Palestine. See now how the church faces this problem: "And the twelve summoned the body of the disciples—that is, the body of the church assembly —and said, 'It is not right that we should give up preaching the word of God to serve tables. Therefore, brethren, pick out from among you seven men of good repute, full of the Spirit and of wisdom, whom we may appoint to this duty. But we will devote ourselves to prayer and to the ministry of the word.' And what they said pleased the whole multitude, and they chose Stephen, a man full of faith and of the Holy Spirit, and Philip and Prochorus, and Nicanor, and Timon, and Parmenas, and Nicolaus, a proselyte of Antioch. These they set before the apostles, and they prayed and laid their hands upon them.

"And the word of God increased; and the number of the disciples multiplied greatly in Jerusalem, and a great many of the priests were obedient to the faith.

"And Stephen, full of grace"—here is another variation; this translation follows some of the oldest and most respected of our ancient manuscripts of the New Testament—full of grace—full of faith, please note, was used in verse 5—"and power, did great wonders and signs among the people."

I want to call your attention to five interesting and

illuminating expressions that appear here with reference to this man Stephen. The first two are found in verse 3 —"full of the Spirit and full of wisdom." The third one is in verse 5—"full of faith." The last two are in verse 8— "full of grace and full of power." These are the five fulnesses, if you will pardon the awkwardness, that are accredited to Stephen by no less an authority than the inspired historian Luke.

Let me remind all of us straight away that the figure at which we are looking is not the figure of an apostle, as was the case when we were looking at Peter. Stephen was a man of the ranks. He was what we should call today, in most church circles, a layman. The New Testament as a whole and the Book of Acts in particular shows us that what is offered to the church is the work of the Holy Spirit, through whom the life of victory and adequacy is as freely offered to lay people as it is to apostles and to ministers. It is God's design and God's desire that all of us should live at floodtide. That is a startling thing to some people: it ought to be an encouraging thing to each of us.

A number of years ago, Dr. William Stidger, a professor of homiletics at one of our seminaries, wrote a book for ministers, to which he gave the fascinating title, *Preaching Out of the Overflow*. The thesis of his book was that in true preaching the preacher never gives the impression that he has only a little that he is capable of saying on the subject, whatever it is. He should always give the impression: "Well now, if I had time, I could go on for *another* thirty minutes, or *another* hour." Preaching out of the overflow!

I should like to take that fine phrase and so broaden

its significance as to apply it to all of life—your life and mine as Christians. We should *live* out of the overflow. In the light of the Book of Acts and other portions of the New Testament, I think we ought to dismiss the idea that there is something about the Christian life that is mean and narrow and cramped and niggardly. Life in Christ is *not* a life with narrow margins around it, in which most of the time you are just barely "getting by," and sometimes not quite "getting by," and down you go in defeat! No! ". . . in all these things we are *more than conquerors* through him who loved us." "God is able to make *all grace* abound toward you, that you *always,* having *all sufficiency,* in *all things"*—right there in that shop where the person next to you is impossibly difficult to get on with; or with that mother-in-law, who can be so awkward (at least you fancy she can!); or with this devastating blow that has crushed you in the permissive providence of God . . . "*always,* having *all sufficiency* in *all things* may *abound* unto every good work."

So Stephen, whose name means "crowned," by the way, is set before us that all of us ordinary people in the ranks of the Christian church may realize that the life of fulness is not simply for missionaries and for pastors, and for bishops, and for church secretaries: the life of overflow is for all of us. Get that, please, from the case of Stephen, this God-crowned, sunlit layman.

It is interesting to observe how Stephen emerges in the Book of Acts. He comes out into the light of day, so to speak, in connection with a problem that arose in the early church soon after the Day of Pentecost, a problem indeed that could have split the church right open. Someone has said that the difference between the first-century church and the twentieth-century church is that the first-century church was power-conscious and the twentieth-century church is problem-conscious. There is a measure of truth in this observation for we are ever talking in our day about the problem of this, and the problem of that, and the problem of the other. However, like many of our generalizations—most of them in point of fact—this one is only a half truth.

It is not true to say, or to imply, that the early church had no problems: it had some very serious and threatening ones. There was the problem of circumcision, for instance: what place to give it among the believers? Here, before us, was a practical problem of administration over which there was a mounting murmur of complaint and protest. "This thing isn't being handled equitably. There is discrimination against some of us." So the complaint ran among some of the widows who received the alms that had been collected. But instead of letting the affair get worse and worse, with growing tensions and the threat of separation, the apostles called the whole church together. They faced it honestly, humbly. And together they sought the guidance of God. Out of that prayerful consultation there arose a decision directed by the Holy Spirit: "Let us not put the responsibility for supervising these temporal matters, this distribution of alms, on the apostles, but let us free them for concentrating on prayer and on the ministry of the Word. Let us select some men right out of the congregation, who stand in the confidence of our people, and who are filled with the Holy Spirit, and give to them this responsibility." Now it was in connection with this decision that there emerged the magnificent figure of this man Stephen.

Mind you, the whole story of Stephen is told in two

chapters of this Book of Acts—chapters 6 and 7. And yet, swift as was his movement across the stage of visible action (such action, that is, as the historian has been led to record for us), he has left behind trailing clouds of glory. He is one of the most admirable figures we have in all the New Testament. It is to him that Luke attributes the fivefold fulness that has arrested our attention: full of the *Holy Spirit,* full of *wisdom,* full of *faith,* full of *grace,* and full of *power.* There was a man "full" for you!

Now he isn't the only man in the world who is full. I know people and you know people who are full enough. The trouble is they are full of the wrong things! The Bible spots some of them. You recall that frightful phrase, "full of bitterness"? People who are gorged with gall! Once in a while you have the misfortune of having to talk to them, and in almost every breath they are exhaling bitterness about something or other. They have just gone sour. They are sour on people, sour on situations, sour on life in general. They are full of bitterness and out it comes in a bitter cascade.

Scripture speaks also of the man who is "full of cursing." There are people like that. I rode with a taxi driver in New York some time ago, and in every other sentence, it seemed, he was using the name of the Lord in vain. After that had gone on for a bit, I said to him, "My dear man, if you knew how it hurts me to hear you speak like that about my friend and my Saviour, the Lord Jesus, I don't believe you would do it." And you know, tough old taxi driver that he was—and New York taxi drivers have a reputation for being tough—he softened immediately. Apologetically he said, "I didn't know I was doing that." And I don't believe he did; he was so full of it that out tumbled his profanities.

Holy Scripture speaks also of those who are "full of confusion" (Job 10:15), of others who are "full of extortion" (Matthew 23:25), of others who are "full of subtlety" (Acts 13:10), and of yet others who are "full of envy, murder, debate, deceit, malignity" (Romans 1:29). They exude evil. They drip with depravity. Stephen, by contrast, appears before us as a man whose fulness of character and life is so gracious and God-like as to leave us forever in debt to Luke for giving us his portrait. Specific features of the portrait must now have our attention.

I

First of all, the fulness we see in Stephen was *inclusive:* he was "full of the Holy Spirit." By that I mean it was *because* Stephen was "full of the Holy Spirit" that he was "full of wisdom" and "full of faith" and "full of grace" and "full of power." I should like to observe with you that being filled with the Holy Spirit is something that is related to the whole of personality and the whole of life. There are people who have the distorted notion that the fulness of the Spirit is simply to deal with some single area of their lives, some one defeat, or some particular weakness. Now it will do that, but may I present to you the bigger, broader, finer, and what I believe to be the more biblical, concept of the fulness of the Holy Spirit in the life of the Christian: as a reality required in order that our *whole* personality may fulfill what Paul calls in Romans 12 "the will of God, what is good and acceptable and perfect."

Join me now in a second observation about the fulness of the Spirit. This is particularly for the benefit of those who haven't given much thought or time or attention to what we might call the theology of the deeper life: the theology of the Holy Spirit, His person and work; the theology of sanctification in the life of the Christian. Many of you have. I thank God for that. But I am speaking, I know, to a considerable number who have not, and for you I should like to make this observation. Do not get the idea that when we speak of the filling of the Holy Spirit, we are thinking of some sensation of being gorged. One meets some people who have the view that if you are really filled, there has to be some kind of emotional ecstasy to register that fact. My dear friends, you can be full of the Spirit of God and have not one scintilla of ecstasy. Indeed you can be full of the Spirit and be passing temporarily through one of those experiences of which Peter speaks when he says, "although now for a season, if need be, ye are in *heaviness* with manifold trails."

No! What we really mean—and the word I am about to use is not the only word that could be used, but I do believe it is a meaningful one and I hope it will be a helpful one—what we really mean is the *control* of the Holy Spirit. He has *got* you, with your consent and no reservations, no bucking, no holding back.

Spelled out, this means a controlled *volitional* life. Your decisions, your choices! A Spirit-filled person doesn't gallop ahead and make decisions without any reference to the mind of Christ or the directing word of the Holy Spirit. No, his choices, especially in all the major concerns of life, are made deliberately under what he is convinced is the direction of the Holy Spirit. You never find a Spirit-filled person saying, "My life is my own and I shall live it as I please." Your life is *not* your own, if you are the Christian God wants you to be. " . . . ye are not your own? . . . ye are bought with a price: therefore glorify God in your body and in your spirit, which are God's" (I Corinthians 6:19,20, KJV).

This means controlled *habits* and *appetites*. The passions need a leash. In themselves they are not evil, but undisciplined, unregulated, unsanctified, they can lead you to fearful sin and the undoing of character.

It means controlled *business practices*. It means controlled *social life* and *recreational activities*.

The fulness of the Holy Spirit! Have you come to the crisis—it doesn't have to be a dramatic crisis, full of emotion, though in some cases it is—in which you actually and honestly acknowledge that you do *not* belong to yourself? God has ordained the paradox: the other side of fulness is emptiness. That which rivals and disputes the Holy Spirit's control, namely this false ego that says "I" independently of God, must be assigned to the cross, there to die. And this, let it be added, is not simply for the Dwight Moodys, the George Müllers, the Hudson Taylors. It is for *all* of us. The story of a layman like Stephen proclaims it.

II

Come now to a second aspect of the fulness that we see in Stephen. It was *perceptive:* he was "full of wisdom." It is a fulness that has insight in it.

The word "wisdom" in the New Testament is used

with varying shades of meaning. In one or two notable passages the whole revelation of God to man in respect of man's salvation in Jesus Christ is revealed by this word. Recall I Corinthians 1:30, which Phillips renders: "Yet from this same God you have received your standing in Jesus Christ, and He has become for us the true Wisdom, a matter, in practice, of being made righteous and holy, in fact, of being redeemed."

Sometimes the word is used quite narrowly as one of the several gifts of the Holy Spirit that Paul deals with in the first Corinthian letter, chiefly in chapters 12 and 14. He speaks of "the word of wisdom," which, Adam Clarke suggests, is particularly linked with the use of the Word of God in bringing men to Christ and to a knowledge of the gospel. Yet another use of the word is found in Ephesians 1:17. Paul speaks of " . . . a spirit of wisdom and of revelation in the knowledge of him, having the eyes of your hearts enlightened. . . . " This, I think, is what God had given to Stephen—a discerning mind, insight. How important it is that you and I should have it! It means sensitiveness to the moods of the Holy Spirit. It means responsiveness to the light and guidance of the Holy Spirit *through the Word*.

Let me catch up that last phrase, if I may, and hold it before you for a moment. I said in the introduction that what we know of Stephen we learn in two chapters of the New Testament, chapters 6 and 7 of this Book of Acts. Now the 7th chapter, you will observe, is a long one—it has sixty verses in it—and it consists largely of an address that Stephen gave to the leaders of the Temple in Jerusalem, who had been guilty of bringing false charges against Jesus, which resulted finally in His death. It is a brave utterance; it is a tremendous utterance; it is an utterance that is all the more remarkable coming from a layman. It is too long for us to print here, but I could wish that all of you would make a point of reading it. For the moment I want to single out just one of its remarkable features. You will find that this is an address given by a man whose mind was saturated with a knowledge of the only Bible that was then available, namely, the Old Testament.

Stephen knew his Bible. He knew Bible characters: Abraham, Isaac, Jacob, Joseph, Moses. He ticked them right off in this address. He knew Bible history: the unfolding of God's purpose through the patriarchs, and through Moses, and through Israel, with her deliverance from the Red Sea, and her formation into an extraordinary nation of worship. Which leads me to remark, if you want to be wise—not in the worldly sense of being clever; you can have a doctorate in philosophy from Harvard or Yale and be very stupid in the things of the Spirit—if you want to be wise, knowledgeable, discerning, in Christian matters, get to know your Bible thoroughly.

The Holy Spirit enlightens and directs those most easily and most surely who know their Bible most thoroughly. That's why it is not enough to know the Bible superficially and fragmentarily. Indeed there is a certain danger in just knowing little bits of your Bible —bits here and bits there. Dr. Campbell Morgan used to warn preachers about the peril of preaching from isolated bits of Scripture. Emphasizing the importance of preaching from context as well as text, he pointed out the danger of using an isolated verse in such a way as to arrive at a wrong conclusion. He would say, "If you let me pick and choose my verses arbitrarily, I can prove anything from the Bible. I can prove that suicide is not only quite legitimate but immediately necessary. I can do it in three verses. My first verse would be, 'Judas went and hanged himself.' My second verse would be, 'Go and do thou likewise.' And my third would be, 'That thou doest, do quickly.'" Now that is all in the Bible and yet it lands you in utter nonsense.

It is particularly risky for persons uninstructed in Holy Scripture to go about saying glibly, "The Holy Spirit guided me to do that." To be sure, the Holy Spirit sometimes guides us through a lonely verse or phrase in the Bible. But it is safer to bear in mind that He guides in keeping with the tenor of Scripture, the total revelation that God has made in His Word. When Satan tried to get at Jesus, in the temptation in the wilderness, he quoted Scripture to Him. Oh, the devil knows the Bible, and he has clever ways, adroit ways, of using it. And our Lord had to come back at him by saying, "Yes, you are correct: that is in Scripture. But Scripture says again. . . . " Scripture balanced with Scripture, Scripture interpreting Scripture—this is what you and I need to know if we are to be wise in the ways and the works and the wonders of our living God. Stephen has set us an admirable example.

III

Come with me to another variety of fulness that is to be seen in this man. His was a _responsive_ fulness: he was "full of faith." What is meant by this phrase? Some would relate it to an expression found in the letter to the Hebrews: ". . . the full assurance of faith . . ." (Hebrews 10:22). It is faith's steadfast confidence, grounded in Scripture and certified by the Holy Spirit in our consciousness, that Christ is in fact, to *us*, the Saviour from sin that He claims to be. Here is assurance, let us sadly acknowledge, that is missing in the lives of many who are presumed to be living in the "household of faith." Yet all are entitled to this confidence, even though the vividness of it may at times be shadowed by illness or depressed emotions.

However, we face here another possibility in interpretation. Let me lead up to it by offering a reminder or two. In the New Testament, faith, seen from one point of view, is a *receiving* thing. It simply takes, gratefully and unworthily. It just receives what Christ has died to make possible for us: our new life in Christ, the pardon of our sins, the fulness of the Holy Spirit. These are gifts that God presents to those who receive them in faith.

But from another point of view, faith is not so much a receiving thing as it is an *achieving* thing: it gets things done: it gets on with the job. Thus we read in verse 8 that Stephen " . . . did great wonders and signs among the people." And in the great classic on faith in the New Testament, the 11th chapter of Hebrews, you remember how you read along till you come to the 32nd verse, and here, if you are like me, somehow you find the tempo of the chronicle picks up and your spirit simply takes wings as you thrill to what the people of God have done through faith: they " . . . conquered kingdoms, enforced justice, received promises, stopped the mouths of lions, quenched raging fire, escaped the edge of the sword,

29

won strength out of weakness, became mighty in war, put foreign armies to flight." Exciting, isn't it? Getting things done in the purpose of God! That is achieving faith. Stephen was full of it.

How is it with you and me? Are we *responding* whole-heartedly to the promises of God? Here is the test. We are too often tempted to think that we are not getting anything done in the exercise of an achieving faith unless it is a sensational, a phenomenal thing. Be willing to start small. Years ago my father was living in Providence, Rhode Island, and journeying every two weeks down to New York for a ministry that God had given him, with a few others who were his colleagues, to the girls of the street in New York City. On one of those trips, a redeemed girl, who hadn't known the Lord very long, full of the joy of her new life, came to him and said, "I know a girl I think I could win if I could get her into a proper environment."

My father said, "Well, have you any place in mind?"

She said, "Yes."

So he said, "Take it."

"But," she said, "I have no money."

He reached into his waistcoat pocket, pulled out a bill and said, "Margaret, take it; take it in the name of the Lord." Do you know, she never forgot that phrase —"Take it in the name of the Lord!" And she not only took the room, but with her faith growing stronger, before she was done, she had taken a whole house, as a place, a home, a Christian center for these girls she was winning for Christ.

Take it in the name of the Lord!

Here is a good question: however far along you may

be in the Christian life, is your faith full enough so that you are taking something—taking a promise, taking a class, taking a mission, taking a stand—for the Lord Christ? Are you bringing something to pass for the glory of the Saviour and the honor of His Kingdom?

> Oh, for trust that brings the triumph,
>   When defeat seems strangely near;
> Oh, for faith that changes fighting
>   Into victory's ringing cheer:
>   Faith triumphant,
>   Knowing not defeat nor fear.

IV

The fulness we see in Stephen has yet another facet. It was an _attractive_ fulness: he was "full of grace" (v. 8).

"If we had been living in Athens in pre-Christian days," Professor Vincent Taylor reminds us, "we should have used the Greek word *charis* quite differently from St. Paul's usage when he speaks of 'the grace of our Lord Jesus Christ.' We should have used the word to describe the *charm* of a lady, the *grace* of a speech, or the *favor* of a king, but not, as St. Paul used it, to describe the free, unmerited love of God, active on our behalf."

The word for *grace*, then, has a background of beauty: it suggests symmetry, rhythm, elegance, loveliness. Paul seized this word as a mold and poured into it a unique Christian content: the matchless excellence of the saving mercy God has extended in Christ to undeserving sinful creatures like ourselves.

Now, what I think can be drawn from this word, as

applied here to Stephen, is a truth that I find fascinating indeed. It is that when the converting, beautifying grace of God in Christ is in fact operative in our hearts, the result is a charm in character which will make itself felt even by those who have no knowledge of its secret source. Thus we read of those who vengefully accused Stephen of misdeeds he had never committed that ". . . gazing at him, all who sat in the council saw that his face was like the face of an angel" (6:15). The radiant beauty of the Master beamed from his eyes, glowed in his countenance, suffused his whole presence and personality.

Was it not John Wesley who said that "one of the advantages of the grace of God is that it makes a man a gentleman without the aid of a dancing master"? In eighteenth century England, I suspect, social dancing was much less a vulgarity and much more a propriety than it is today. Parents wishing their children to acquire proper manners and social grace hired the services of dancing masters. "Well," said Mr. Wesley, in whom there was a well-knit synthesis of the Puritan, the Spartan, and the Christian, "if the grace of the Saviour possesses you, you can pocket the money you might give to the terpsichorean tutors, or, better still, give it to God and His Church."

The radiance of Christ in Stephen—it challenged his foes and charmed his friends. Sanctity doesn't have to be gushy to be attractive. Indeed the real thing is not gushy. Its winsomeness is never forced, never strained, never affected.

Perhaps we should all ask ourselves: Has anybody been round lately, saying, "I want what you have!" Has the *shortage* of grace made us repel people, or has the *overflow* of grace allured them—to the Saviour from whom it comes?

You perhaps have heard the story of the Salvation Army lassie and the sour-visaged man whom she took for a prospective convert, when he was in fact an office-bearer in one of the churches. An open-air meeting was in progress, and the grim-looking gentleman stood at the rim of the listening crowd. The eager lassie asked, "Are you saved?"

The acidity of his reply was intended to conceal his embarrassment. The words he bit off were: "I hope I am."

As reported, the girl, with less tact than zeal, called out to the leader of the meeting: "He says that he *hopes* he is saved. *What a face for a child of God!*" Tact or no tact, you can't imagine her ever saying that about Stephen, can you?

V

We move now to the final aspect of fulness seen in this grace-crowned man. It was an *effective* fulness: he was "full of power" (v. 8).

We live in a power-hungry and power-conscious age. We have schemes and structures of power—political, economic, military—that are quite fantastic. Yet a certain futility is the curse of them all: they fail to infuse us with the most meaningful power of all, which is precisely the ability to *live* as the Creator-Redeemer God intends His creatures to live. Hordes of humans, including many Christians, simply do not demonstrate the power that deals redemptively with such basic human ills as self-centeredness, quarrelsomeness, resentfulness, fretfulness, lovelessness, and fearfulness. Full of ideas— and of ideals as well? Yes, certainly. Full of good intentions, hopes, and promises? Yes. Full of cleverness, or suavity, or charm? Yes. But obviously—and pathetically —*not* full of power!

But Stephen was. Indisputably, he *was!*

Look at it, I beg you, in its specific release:

Power *for proclamation*—the Spirit of God poured *that* through Stephen. ". . . you shall receive power," Jesus promised, "when the Holy Spirit has come upon you; and you shall be my witnesses . . . " (Acts 1:8). Now it was being fulfilled in the testimony that Stephen gives before the hostile leaders of the Temple. "We need to remember," says Paget Wilkes in *The Dynamic of Service,* "that the convicting power on the day of Pentecost was poured through no eloquent lips of magnificent discourse. It rather flowed along the new-cut watercourses of simple testimony."

In this case the flowing stream of witness became a torrent of testimony joined with admonition. I speak to you, cried Stephen, of " . . . the Righteous One, whom you have now betrayed and murdered" (7: 52). It was potent stuff, combining, as it did, conviction, courage, and spiritual authority.

But now observe, further, that the power of the Holy Spirit in this man was not only for proclamation: it was power *under persecution.* How the Christian *acts* is one test of spiritual adequacy, to be sure. It is not the only test, however. How the Christian *reacts* is an equally significant test. In a semi-slang manner of speaking, we

34

may have power to *give it,* but do we have power to *take it?* There are times when the strength to *express* ourselves for Christ must be matched by the strength silently to *endure* for Christ. No back talk, no recrimination, no clamorous self-defense—just bearing it, as Jesus did before Herod!

In the midst of his witness Stephen was howled down. "Now when they heard these things they were enraged, and they ground their teeth against him." (v. 54).

And his reaction? Here it is: "But he, full of the Holy Spirit, gazed into heaven and saw the glory of God, and Jesus standing at the right hand of God" (v. 55). They had the capacity to be enraged—and it was devilish; he had the capacity to endure—and it was divine.

Their fury rose to a madness, mob-like and murderous: "But they cried out with a loud voice and stopped their ears and rushed together upon him. Then they cast him out of the city and stoned him . . . " (vv. 57, 58).

And now comes the ultimate in Holy Spirit power. Power for proclamation is required. Power under persecution is at times an essential. But the ultimate is *power in prayer.* "And as they were stoning Stephen, he prayed, 'Lord Jesus, receive my spirit'" (v. 59). This was the prayer for himself. But he didn't finish with himself in view.

Listen!

"And he knelt down and cried with a loud voice, 'Lord, do not hold this sin against them'" (v. 60). Who that heard it could ever forget it—this prayer of unretaliating good will for his murderers? Young Saul of Tarsus was looking on, and he never forgot it.

That reeling, battered form, absorbing blows against which his hands held no defense but over which his spirit was exultantly triumphant! That prayer so like the prayer of the dying Saviour that the similarity spoke not of coincidence but of communion!

That upturned face, shining with a light never seen on land or sea!

The waiting Saviour! The Eternal Portals wide open! And the God-filled man was no more.

For God had taken him!

3 Barnabas:

The Man Who Made Goodness Attractive

TEXT: *"he was a good man, full of the
Holy Spirit and of faith . . ."*
Acts 11:24.

AS WE TURN again to the Book of Acts for our study
of God's actors, I hope that already you have begun
to realize—some for the first time, others in a fresh
way—how kind God is in His Word to us. He has
different ways of getting the truth across to us. In the
New Testament we have history to inform us, and we
have doctrine to instruct us, but we have also examples
to inspire us.

The renowned Prime Minister Gladstone once said
that one example is worth a thousand arguments. The
Lord seems to say to us, "Through My inspired servants
I give you in the Gospels a bit of My biography, and
in the Epistles I take you into My classroom; but here

in the Acts I want you to walk with Me through My picture gallery. I want to show you how this all works out. I want to show you that this can be *lived*, this great teaching of Christlikeness and witness and adequacy and usefulness." We must see for ourselves how God can take frail and unworthy men and women and boys and girls, and work through them after the fashion of His working through the lives of these men whom we see in the Book of Acts

So to the portrait of Barnabas we turn now. Barnabas whom our Lord used to make goodness attractive! We are first introduced to Barnabas in chapter 4. We found that the portrait of Stephen was a compact and tidy one; it is all in two chapters right together, 6 and 7. But Barnabas pops in and out of the Book of Acts, and so we have to move around a bit to get the full portrait. In chapter 4, vv. 36 and 37 we read, ". . . Joseph who was surnamed by the apostles Barnabas (which means, Son of encouragement), a Levite, a native of Cyprus, sold a field which belonged to him, and brought the money and laid it at the apostles' feet." That is our introduction to this man.

Chapter 9, as you will remember, gives us the thrilling story of the conversion of Saul of Tarsus, the man who had been such a rabid and relentless foe of the Christian movement, who had been so cruel to the Christians themselves; but who, on one of his expeditions of persecution, was suddenly confronted by the risen Saviour and his conversion took place. This was up in the north country, you remember, near Damascus. Now the newly converted Saul of Tarsus has come down to Jerusalem, and we read at verse 26: "And when he had come to

Jerusalem he attempted to join the disciples; and they were all afraid of him, for they did not believe that he was a disciple. But Barnabas took him and brought him to the apostles, and declared to them how on the road he"—Paul—"had seen the Lord, who spoke to him, and how at Damascus he had preached boldly in the name of Jesus. So"—that is, with the sponsoring that Barnabas gave him—"so he [Paul] went in and out among them at Jerusalem. . . . "

Then in chapter 11, we have an extremely interesting and important development in the ongoing story of the Book of Acts, in the building, the development, the expansion of the Christian church and the Christian movement. Following the martyrdom of Stephen, there was a fierce outbreak of persecution against the Christians in the Jerusalem area. Accordingly, at verse 19 of chapter 11 we read: "Now those who were scattered because of the persecution that arose over Stephen traveled as far as Phoenicia and Cyprus and Antioch, speaking the word to none except Jews. But there were some of them, men of Cyprus and Cyrene, who on coming to Antioch spoke to the Greeks also, preaching the Lord Jesus. And the hand of the Lord was with them, and a great number that believed turned to the Lord. News of this came to the ears of the church in Jerusalem, and they sent Barnabas to Antioch. When he came and saw the grace of God, he was glad; and he exhorted them all to remain faithful to the Lord with steadfast purpose; for he was a good man, full of the Holy Spirit and of faith. And a large company was added to the Lord. So Barnabas went to Tarsus to look for Saul; and when he had found him, he brought him to Antioch. For a whole year they met with the church, and taught a large company of people; and in Antioch the disciples were for the first time called Christians."

Now our key word for this study, as you may have guessed, is the word that is recorded in v. 24 of this 11th chapter: *"for he was a good man, full of the Holy Spirit and of faith."*

I

THE DIFFICULTY WE FACE

I think that straight away it might be helpful if we took notice of the word "good," or "goodness," to use it as a noun. It is a word widely misunderstood, most often outside Christian circles in what we call the world, but sometimes even within Christian circles. So far as the worldly mind is concerned, there is a great deal of cynicism about this matter of goodness. It is the cynic that says, "Well, I don't believe anybody can be good anyhow; and even if people could be good, they wouldn't be very attractive." Cynics of this variety have in mind certain people who, though super-sanctimonious, are sour and awkward and repulsive. The cynical objector is therefore "fed up" with the whole thing.

Of if they don't quite take that view of it, there are detractors whose cynicism is a kind of sordid thing that frankly and even vulgarly says, "Well, after all, goodness isn't interesting. If you want to live a dull life, just be good!"

I was in a public library some time ago, looking at a shelf of psychology books, taking one down and then another, just to see what they were like. I was struck with the title of one of them, *Why We Can't Be Good.* On the flyleaf there was a quotation which evidently spoke the temper of the author's mind. It read: "Sin writes history; goodness is silent." I was reminded of a passage in one of the books of the late Dr. John Gossip of Scotland: "It is held by many as a first axiom that holiness is a dull affair, and God's company intolerably dreary, and that for vividness and color and interest you must look elsewhere." That is the attitude of a vast number of people in the world. You and I must realize that if we are going to be seriously Christian, we must set our minds against this current of skeptical thought and cynical sentiment.

More surprising, however, is another misunderstanding we have in some circles regarding goodness. It is a kind of theological twist in which, on very serious doctrinal grounds, we deny that even in the Christian scheme of things people can be made good. For example, I sometimes hear ministers, attempting to support this negative position, bring St. Paul to their side with what is presumed to be a proof-text. It is taken from the 3rd chapter of Romans, which in the Authorized Version, reads: "There is none that doeth good, no, not one." It is worth our pausing just for a moment while I try to show you that here is an example of what I was touching on, from another point of view, earlier: how wrong you can be if you do not take Scripture in context. The whole 3rd chapter of Romans is Paul's indictment of the entire world, Jew and Gentile, outside of Christ. It is not a description of the community of the redeemed, or of the character of the redeemed. It is a description of the

41

world in its lostness, outside of Christ. It is therefore poor exposition, if you take this clause, "There is none that doeth good, no, not one" and exclaim, "Now there it is. If you say that Christians can really be good, you aren't Pauline in your teaching!"

Perhaps it will help you to see clearly for yourself the point of what I am saying if you take the paragraph here in Romans 3, and just insert the word "Christian" again and again. You will see how absurd it makes Paul's statement. Begin with verse 10: "There is not a Christian that is righteous, no, not one; no Christian understands; not one Christian seeks for God. All Christians have turned aside, together they have gone wrong; not one Christian is good, no not one. Their Christian throat is an open grave; they use their Christian tongues to deceive; the venom of asps is under their Christian lips. Their Christian mouth is full of curses and bitterness. Their Christian feet are swift to shed blood, and in their Christian paths are ruin and misery, and the way of peace these Christians do not know. There is no fear of God before their Christian eyes."

You see how ridiculous that is. No, this is Paul's way of saying that no matter who we are, Jew or Gentile, cultured or illiterate, we all have sinned and come short of the glory of God, and we are all in need therefore of that redeeming grace, that forgiving and life-changing mercy, which Jesus Christ has purchased so dearly for us by His death and the shedding of His blood upon the cross.

Having said all that, may I now say that when Barnabas is described as a "good man," it is not in the sense that he was *naturally* good or *inherently* good or *legal-*

istically good. Not at all. It is in the sense, rather, that he had allowed Jesus Christ to come with His own life and pardon and righteousness, and transfigure him by His own dwelling within him. It is *Christian* goodness, which is Christ-within goodness. What a wonderful thing it is to take Christian goodness, the goodness that is ours not by nature but by grace, and through the working of Christ's Holy Spirit within us, so manifest it that it becomes attractive in our neighborhood and in our families and in the society of others! That is what we see in Barnabas. Let's trace it out.

II

THE DESCRIPTION WE FIND

Now if you had been an associate or a colleague of Barnabas in the church, or maybe a non-Christian observer of Barnabas, what *would* you have seen? What in particular would have made this Christian goodness attractive to you? What we see exhibited by grace in Barnabas is the goodness of a *generous* spirit. Thus, in chapter 4, we are told that Barnabas, who was a Levite —this in verses 36 and 37—". . . a native of Cyprus, sold a field which belonged to him, and brought the money and laid it at the apostles' feet."

Barnabas, you see, had a *stewardship* rather than an *ownership* view of property. We need an hour on the subject of stewardship alone, and we can devote only two or three minutes to it here. May I say to all of us, old and young alike, that nobody is really good in the Christian sense who is mean and miserly and grasping;

who is ungenerous with Christ, and His church, and His broken world. The goodness of Barnabas, contrariwise, flowered in this magnificent demonstration of Christian stewardship.

Actually, it's a bit singular that Barnabas should be described here as a Levite. Why do I say singular? Because originally the Levites were not permitted to have any property at all. That was God's order, you remember, when the children of Israel got into the land of Canaan, and they parceled it out. Zebulon had this district in Canaan, and Issacher had that, and so on with Dan and Judah, Asher and the rest. But Levites were not to have any territory. Why? Because they were the priestly tribe, and they were to live on the tithes of all the people of Israel.

But in the passing of the years things had changed greatly, and especially in the "between-Testaments" period, the 400 years between the close of the Old Testament and the beginning of the New. Many ancient observances in Israel had been by-passed, glossed over, ignored. Thus in the passing of time, Levites became not only property-holders but sometimes, as in the case of Barnabas, wealthy landed gentry, after the old manner of many Christians in Great Britain: owners of vast estates, with castles and servants, and horses and hounds, and much else that they had in their name and at their command. This is pretty largely a thing of the past, if I am correctly informed. In any case, perhaps Barnabas would have qualified for a place among these gentry.

Now, however, the great change had come in Barnabas' life. Christ had his heart, and He had made it big and generous. Barnabas sold his property, brought the

44

money, and laid it at the apostles' feet. Such was his lavish generosity towards Christ and His church! The amount of money you have, or the amount of property, is not the determining thing in Christian stewardship. It is your attitude toward it. Do you really believe it isn't yours? Do you really believe it is God's and that you are only a trustee?

If yours is a Christ-created goodness, you are concerned about taking a Christian attitude towards the *making* of money. That means that as an employer you are generous in the way you treat your employees. You don't grind them or exploit them. You treat them justly and magnanimously. A steward, moreover, is careful about the way he *spends* his money. Again, you see, it is not his except in a secondary sense. He is the trustee of it; it belongs to God. And "it is required in stewards," says St. Paul, "that a man be found faithful."

In Ceylon is a distinguished church leader by the name of D. T. Niles. Years ago he was a pastor in Ceylon's northern city, Jaffna, where one of his duties was to go every month to the home of a widow whose husband had been a pastor, and to give her a little monthly pension from the church fund. It was five rupees a month, a rupee being worth roughly twenty cents. He said that every three months when he made this call, after he had given her her five rupees, she would cross the room, take down something like a handkerchief, untie it, and hand over to him a certain number of annas—the tithe of her tiny monthly allowance. She would say, "Pastor, take this for the Lord's work." And Dr. Niles said, "I never received the money without inwardly thanking God for such devotion, such dedication, on the part of one of His children." Here, you will agree, was an alluringly beautiful Christ-induced goodness.

But the goodness that we see so attractively embodied by grace in this man Barnabas has another aspect: he was a man with a *magnanimous* spirit. This is especially true where people are concerned. Let's dip into this 9th chapter a moment, and come sharply to the point. Here is the case of Saul of Tarsus, famous for his opposition to the Christian cause, and tireless, relentless in his persecution of the Christians. But now, yonder in Damascus, he has been converted; he has begun to witness for Christ. Then he journeys down to Jerusalem and wants to be received into the fellowship of the Christians there. But they are afraid of him! When he attempts to join the disciples, they are all suspicious of him! They hold him at arm's length. Now this next clause is a shocker! I think it ought to cause all of us to search our hearts. Even though it is a bit of a digression it is worth noticing in passing: " . . . for they did not believe he was a disciple." My word, hadn't they been praying that he would become a Christian? And now that he had, they wouldn't believe it! How many of you have prayed that Mr. Brezhnev might be converted? I must confess that I have done very little praying about it—some, quite honestly, but not as much as I should have. Are we to believe that anybody is outside the pale? God forgive us if we do. And this, I think, was almost like Mr. Brezhnev coming to your church and saying, "I'd like to join your fellowship!" Perhaps you would be a Barnabas about it, but I wonder! I fear there are some who would lift their eyebrows, and, mastered by suspicion, would say, "Now what's he got up his sleeve?" Well, that's the way they treated Saul.

However—next verse—"But Barnabas took him"—a newly converted man and the whole lot of them in Jerusalem saying, "Oh no. We can't receive you!" "But Barnabas took him and brought him to the apostles, and declared to them how on the road he had seen the Lord, who spoke to him, and how at Damascus he had preached boldly in the name of Jesus." A magnanimous soul, who wasn't going to hold a new convert at arm's length; who wasn't going to be unforgiving towards him because he, Paul, had been so cruel to the Christians! God forgive us that sometimes we Christians who are so evangelical in our theology can be so enameled in our sympathy—hard and unforgiving toward people who have sinned. Barnabas was large-hearted in his treatment of a man who needed acceptance and couldn't get it.

But this magnanimity, mark you, carried on beyond this point. Look at the 11th chapter. Here is this Christian movement that has begun in Antioch. Many had turned to the Lord. We read in verse 22: "News of this came to the ears of the church in Jerusalem, and they sent Barnabas to Antioch. When he came and saw the grace of God, he was glad. . . ." Now, mind you, here was a mixed bag; for earlier in this 11th chapter some of these believers were Jews who had confessed Christ as Messiah and Saviour, and some were Gentiles; so it is to be presumed that here there would be some of the same tensions and problems as there were between the Jewish believers and the Gentile believers in Jerusalem. It was an awkward situation in which the

Jerusalem leaders said, "Barnabas, you go. You have a ministry with these people." He wasn't an apostle, but they knew he had the right spirit.

He went. He saw Christian reality, and he was glad. But he saw something else. He saw that this thing was too big for him: it was too much for him to manage. So, after reading as we do in the last part of verse 24, "And a large company was added to the Lord," in the next verse we read, "So Barnabas went to Tarsus to look for Saul." For about nine years, as nearly as we can calculate, Saul had been out of sight, since his conversion. He was being seasoned. And now Barnabas, with a situation on his hands which thrills him on the one hand and awes him on the other, seems to say, "This is too big a job for me. I'm perfectly willing to put my oar in and do what I can, but I need help. I know where there's a man who has got what this situation needs. I am going to go and get Paul."

Now you know, a smaller man, a meaner man, would not have done that. I'm afraid I have met even some preachers who would have said, "Oh boy, I'm going to be a big duck in the puddle! I've got this all to myself!" But not Barnabas! He wanted to take a man who he knew was a first-class scholar, steeped in the Old Testament, well read in philosophy, and now, above all, a follower of Jesus Christ. He said, "Paul is the man to cope with the difficulties and the possibilities that belong to this situation in Antioch. I'll stand by him and hold up his hands, and we'll work this out together." That was the magnanimity of Barnabas!

Don't be so vocal with your fundamentalism, don't be so garrulous about your evangelicalism, if at the same

48

time you have such a mean, cramped heart that you have to have the limelight for yourself. One of the signs of Christian goodness is that you don't get miffed if you have to play second fiddle! Christ had stamped big-souled Barnabas with precisely such a mark.

There are other things I should like to say on that point, but I want you to see another manifestation of the Christian goodness of this man Barnabas: he was a man with an *infectious* spirit. He was contagiously encouraging wherever he went. Now I said we would have to do a bit of switching back and forth in following Barnabas through Acts. I must take you back a moment to chapter 4. At verse 36 there is a touch in the narrative that we want: "Thus Joseph who was surnamed by the apostles Barnabas (which means, Son of encouragement. . . ." Ah! Then Barnabas was not the name his father and mother had given him. They had named him Joseph. But those who got to know him well in Christian relationships, in Christian intimacy, said, "We must give this man another name!" For everywhere Barnabas went he had a genius for lifting the mood and the spirit of the people. This son of encouragement was adept at saying the right word, putting the right pressure into the handclasp, flashing the right light in a smile or a nod, conveying the right impulse in a phrase or sentence of sympathy. A son of consolation!

You see, Barnabas did not have the genius that *scintillates*. Paul had that. Barnabas had just the genius that *serves*. He was contagiously happy and helpful. You have discovered that some people, when they come around and talk with you, depress you. You don't like to be rude, but when they leave you say, "Well, thank the

49

Lord, they're gone!" What little morale you did have when they came has been taken right away from you. They left you with a weight on your spirit and no wings. Faultfinding, critical, hard, gloomy—such was their temper.

But then there are other people who, when they come around, do not have to be with you five minutes till they have shot sunshine through your whole spirit; they have kindled you. Hopes were down; they have lifted them. Courage was pretty largely gone; they have put new heart and boldness into you.

Ah yes! It's a wonderful thing to let the radiant goodness of Christ express itself through you, as it did through Barnabas. As a consequence the ministry of helpfulness becomes not a thing forced or put on, but unaffected and unshadowed.

Among the gifts of the Spirit that Paul discusses in I Corinthians 12, there are such endowments as the gift of tongues, and the Corinthians, as we know, were fond of it, fascinated by it. They wanted to speak in tongues, or perform miracles. Paul's teaching on the gifts, you will remember, is that no one of them is possessed by all believers. They are divided severally as the Spirit wills. Now there is one gift that I have known only one person in my ministry to covet. (St. Paul holds that the gifts are covetable, especially the more useful ones, even though they are not surely promised.) The gift I have in mind is the one called "helps," or "helpers," as it is in the Revised Standard Version. I have known people who coveted the gift of tongues, and many who have desired the gift of healing; and I used to say that I had never known of anyone coveting the gift of helps.

But one day a young lady came to me and said, "My mother prayed for that gift!" Just to be a helper! "Miracles" on one side and "administrations" on the other—(bishops and presidents and moderators!) And sandwiched in between—just *helps!* The helper is somebody who knows how to get into the chinks, into the out-of-the-way places: somebody who knows how to write a letter that reaches a discouraged Christian just in time; somebody who knows how to send over a meal to a family that is hungry! A son of encouragement!

Years ago I came on the phrase, "the fine art of making goodness attractive." It was this Christian art in which Barnabas was skilled. Have you ever heard of the prayer of the little girl who at the family devotions said, "Lord, make the bad people good, and Lord, please make the good people nice!" That's what we want. Good people made nice! A kind of goodness that is not repulsive but attractive! Barnabas had it.

And then I must briefly point out that Barnabas was blessed with a *solicitous* spirit. This too belongs to the fruitage of goodness as we see it in this man's Christian soul. Barnabas was solicitous for those in need of a Saviour. For we read here, in connection with our text, "for he was a good man, full of the Holy Spirit and of faith. And a large company was added to the Lord" (v. 24). He found a goodly company of believers when he came, but when he had ministered to them and had witnessed to others concerning Christ, even though he did not have the gifts of Paul, more were added to the Lord.

Christian goodness is evangelistic. I don't mean to say that you have to be a Billy Graham. But I do

51

mean that every Christian should be solicitous about the conversion to Christ of those in his family, his pals, his office associates, his professional colleagues. Don't say that Christian goodness has come to flower in your life unless there is a loving concern for the evangelization of the lonely, alien, broken world for which Jesus Christ bled upon the cross.

But I am not content with that statement. When I say "world," the danger is that it will sound impersonal. Concern for people—that, too, is our crying need in the ranks of Christians. "When one thinks of the zeal of a convinced Communist," wrote Dr. W. E. Sangster in *Let Me Commend,* "or the hot enthusiasm of certain social philosophers running round with their latest nostrum to cure the world's ills, how strange it is that we can be so tepid in our vital task!" In the famous Myers' poem, *St. Paul,* the apostle, looking sensitively into the lives of those alienated from Christ, cried out:

Then with a rush the intolerable craving
Shivers through me like a trumpet call—
Oh, to save these! To perish for their saving,
Die for their life, be offered for them all!

III

THE DYNAMIC WE FEEL

The generous, magnanimous, infectious, solicitous spirit we have discovered in Barnabas was not something of his own making. The power that explains it was the power of God, and it was operative in this dear man because he appropriated it. Thus we read, in our key verse: "he was . . . full of the Holy Spirit and of faith."

You *feel* this as you expose yourself to the life and work of this lay leader in the early church. You feel freshness, not staleness; fearlessness, not frustration, aggressiveness, not complacency; passion, not paleness.

Two things are brilliantly clear in Acts, it seems to me: (1) that the fulness of the Holy Spirit, the being utterly surrendered to and cleansed by, the Spirit, is the key to spiritual power; and (2) that this fulness may be had by any Christian, or, corporately speaking, by a whole company of Christians in unity, if only we will decisively take hold of it and begin to act upon the faithfulness of God with respect to it.

Henry Drummond made the observation that "in the New Testament alone the Spirit is referred to nearly three hundred times. And the one word with which He is constantly associated is Power." You feel that as you study Barnabas. You feel it too as you rub shoulders with laymen today who have struck out from the shallow, marginal waters of the Spirit and have plunged into the central stream. Listen to the testimony of a university undergraduate who had done just this. He writes to Dr. Samuel Shoemaker:

What a life! Being in God's hands is the most wonderful home imaginable. What a lesson I am learning—do you remember the despondent character of my last few letters? The Lord was teaching me something: that I don't have Christianity, Christ has me. Man, the faithfulness of God! It's the most wonderful revelation. Your letters and books, constant prayer, reading, and fellowship, plus the wonderful power of the Holy Spirit, are all combining to show me so convincingly that God's love is faithful and abiding. . . . My girl's roommate has just become a Christian. We've been praying for her for almost two years. I saw her last week, and she was so hungry. I gave her *How to Become A Christian*, and the Holy Spirit took over. What a thrill!"

Here too one gets the *feeling* that a Christian dynamic not derivable from man is potently at work, leading Dr. Shoemaker to exclaim, "Why are there not more men like this—strong, a fine athlete—being produced by our work in colleges, and our Young People's groups at home?"

The Barnabas fraternity is in need of enlargement. It is open to those who, with no goodness of their own, will let the good Redeemer employ them to make His goodness attractive.

> The Lord, who left the heavens
>   Our life and peace to bring,
> To dwell in lowliness with men,
>   Their pattern and their King:
>
> He to the lowly soul
>   Doth still Himself impart,
> And for His dwelling and His throne
>   Chooseth the pure in heart.

4 Philip:

The Man Who Could Fade Out Gracefully

TEXT: "... and they chose ... Philip. ..." Acts 6:5.

I DO HOPE this exciting Book of Acts is beginning to be alive in a new way for you as we approach it from the point of view of these remarkable personalities whose story is told, in greater or less detail, in the book itself—God's actors in the Book of Acts. In this chapter we are concerned with a man by the name of Philip. There are two Philips, as you know, in the New Testament: there are Philip the Apostle and the one who is rather familiarly known as Philip the Evangelist. It is the Evangelist who comes before us now.

I want at the outset to take a look at a brief word in chapter 6, where Philip emerges for the first time. We have already been in chapter 6, you will remember, for our study of Stephen. It happens that Stephen and Philip became colleagues among those "serving men" that were chosen by the early church in Jerusalem after the congregation got into difficulties over the inequitable distribution of the alms given to the needy members of the church, particularly to the widows. In the crisis that arose it was decided that there should be this group of ministrants or servers. The Greek word is *deacon*. The term "deacon," however, can be confusing in our day, for the simple reason that we have bodies of Christians in which the office of deacon is an order of the clergy. This is true both of Anglicans and Methodists. In other communions the diaconate is for the laity. It would be in this sense that we should think of Philip as a deacon.

Thus we see these seven men in the Jerusalem church appointed and dedicated for the task of distributing the benevolence of the congregation. It is in a context such as this that we first come upon Philip. We read in verse 5 of chapter 6, "And what they said pleased the whole multitude, and they chose Stephen, a man full of faith and of the Holy Spirit, and Philip. . . ." So we have Philip appearing as a layman out of the ranks, so full of the Holy Spirit and so highly respected by the congregation that he was entrusted with this newly defined and important responsibility.

Now come to chapter 8. Here is where we have the fullest account of Philip and his life and work. Let's begin with the 4th verse. "Now those who were scattered went about preaching the word. Philip went down to a city of Samaria, and proclaimed to them the Christ. And the multitudes with one accord gave heed to what was said by Philip, when they heard him and saw the signs which he did. For unclean spirits came out of many who were possessed, crying with a loud voice; and many who were paralyzed or lame were healed. So there was much joy in that city."

Move on to verse 26. But—right in the midst of this wonderful mission in Samaria—". . . an angel of the Lord said to Philip, 'Rise and go toward the south to the road that goes down from Jerusalem to Gaza.' This is a desert road. And he rose and went. And behold, an Ethiopian, a eunuch, a minister of Candace, the queen of the Ethiopians, in charge of all her treasure, had come to Jerusalem to worship and was returning; seated in his chariot, he was reading the prophet Isaiah. And the Spirit said to Philip, 'Go up and join this chariot.' So Philip ran to him, and heard him reading Isaiah the prophet, and asked, 'Do you understand what you are reading?' And he said, 'How can I, unless some one guides me?' And he invited Philip to come up and sit with him. Now the passage of scripture which he was reading was this:

As a sheep led to the slaughter
or a lamb before its shearer is dumb,
so he opens not his mouth.
In his humiliation justice was denied him.
Who can describe his generation?
For his life is taken up from the earth.'

And the eunuch said to Philip, 'About whom, pray, does the prophet say this, about himself or about some one else?' Then Philip opened his mouth, and beginning with this scripture he told him the good news of Jesus. And as they went along the road they came to some water, and the eunuch said, 'See, here is water! What is to prevent my being baptized?" And he commanded the chariot to stop, and they both went down into the water, Philip and the eunuch, and he baptized him. And when they came up out of the water, the Spirit of the Lord caught up Philip; and the eunuch saw him no more, and went on his way rejoicing. But Philip was found at Azotus, and passing on he preached the gospel to all the towns till he came to Caesarea."

The text of the Revised Standard Version omits the words—"And Philip said, 'If you believe with all your heart, you may'; and he replied, 'I believe that Jesus Christ is the Son of God.'" Now this is given in the Revised only as a marginal reading, the reason being that there are some ancient and highly respected manuscripts which omit it. I rather like to have it in.

Our final reference in the Book of Acts requires us to turn page after page, till we come to chapter 21. Here we find St. Paul on his way to Jerusalem for the last time, returning from his missionary journey; and on the way he stops in the city of Caesarea. Thus we read in verse 8, "On the morrow"—and here Luke includes himself with Paul and their traveling companions—". . . we departed and came to Caesarea, and we entered the house of Philip the evangelist, who was one of the seven, and stayed with him. And he had four unmarried daughters who prophesied." The years have gone, and here is Philip in retirement. Not idle, I dare say, but on the other hand no longer in the heat of action. No crowds waiting on his ministry! No dramatic episodes of winning a cabinet member to Christ! More, in fact, to be said about his daughters than about him!

Philip, the man who could fade out gracefully! I want

to take this topic in three stages. There are three phases in Philip's career, which may be likened to the stages of the day. First, I want us to see Philip in the *dawnlight*. Then, Philip in the *noonlight*. Last, Philip in the *twilight*.

THE DAWNLIGHT

We begin by looking at Philip at the commencement of his recorded Christian activity. As we have already seen, he comes to the fore in connection with a new development in the policy and practice of the early Christian church, where the apostles, the twelve, said in effect, "Let our hands be freed from this responsibility of looking after the temporal, the economic, needs of our widows, and let us have men who are specially appointed for this purpose." So they chose the seven, one of whom was Philip.

There are two observations on this that I think are worth while: a) The first one is that Philip symbolizes the place of significant usefulness that Christ, the head of the church, has for every one of us in His body. When we had the Reformation under Martin Luther and others, it seems a pity that in some respects the Reformers failed to go far enough. While we talk about the priesthood of all believers as one of the cardinal principles of the reformed Christian faith, still in most of our Protestant communions of the last two or three hundred years we have not had a clear understanding that the laity are as truly and as fully the servants of Christ in the church, and therefore responsible for its

59

work, as are the ministers. Only now, in Europe and America, are our Protestant groups coming to a recognition of what we have been missing—this unused, unmobilized, Christian manpower among our laity.

In the Church of Scotland, for example, particularly in connection with the Tell Scotland Movement, they have begun to popularize a phrase I like. They speak of the "apostolate of the laity." The apostolate of the *laity!* After all, the word "laity" comes from a Greek word which means *the people;* and "apostle" comes from a word which means simply *sent.* Remember, it was not to the twelve only—or the eleven, as it was before Matthias was chosen—that our Lord was speaking, but to the *whole* church, when He said, "As the Father hath sent Me so have I sent you." I have apostled you! And I should like my lay friends to be reminded that it is just as much your responsibility to carry out the great commission of Jesus, and evangelize this word with His gospel, as it is my responsibility.

b) There is a second observation suggested by the case of Philip as we see him here in the dawnlight of his ministry. It is this: when he was chosen with the other six to look after the temporal, material interests and well-being of certain members of the church, we are not to think that this was an unspiritual task. To put my thoughts positively, here was an area of activity that was just as spiritual as was the preaching of the Word by Peter or, later, by Paul. Again, I wish I could say something to encourage our lay people to believe that serving in capacities in the church in which they have to handle money, or deal with administrative problems, or even serve as a sexton and sweep out the church and keep it tidy—that this, when it is done unto the Saviour and in the power of His Holy Spirit, is as spiritual a service as preaching a sermon or leading a prayer. This is what Philip says to us right here in the dawnlight of his remarkable life.

The late Dr. Stuart Holden, in a book of his that I read when I was just a young minister, tells of something that occurred when he was in Africa. Being introduced to an African Christian one day, he asked him, "What do you do, my brother?"

Quick as a wink the man replied, "I am a cabinetmaker to the glory of God!" Exactly! When you are a cabinetmaker, or a butcher, or a baker, or a farmer, or a secretary, or a housewife, or a labor union officer, or a manufacturer, or a legislator, *to the glory of God*, you are not doing a secular work, you are doing a spiritual work. Please draw that lesson from Philip.

II

THE NOONLIGHT

Now we are to see Philip in the glare of midday. He is right out on the open stage of tremendous, even dramatic, public action and service. This takes us to the 8th chapter. There are three things that I want you to see in Philip, as he appears here so prominently and so splendidly in the work of God. First, we shall see him as a man flexibly in touch with the Holy Spirit; second, as a man firmly in touch with the gospel; and third, as a man fondly in touch with people.

a) First, then, here is a man who is *flexibly in touch*

with the Holy Spirit. You will remember that one of the qualifications for the selection of these seven serving men, or deacons, was that they were to be "full of the Holy Spirit": not simply given new life by the Spirit of God but enabled by the Spirit to express that life cleanly and conqueringly. We are now about to see what happens in the life of a layman whom the Holy Spirit thus controls, as this man moves out from a limited sphere of action in the mother church in Jerusalem to a totally new scene where God is going to use him astonishingly. William Barclay, of Glasgow, in his commentary on the Acts of the Apostles, does not hesitate to call Philip one of the architects of the Christian church: so high a place does he give him.

Now what do we have in mind when we describe Philip as a man *flexibly* in the hands of the Holy Spirit? We mean at least two things: For one thing, we mean that he was open and fluid as to how he might be led by the Spirit. This is important; it is important for young Christians to learn. We so easily develop certain rigid ideas about the Spirit-guided and the Spirit-controlled life. We suppose that because the Spirit has dealt with us one way one time, He is under obligation to deal with us the same way next time. And He is not! Philip was wise enough and well-taught enough to realize that this was the case, and not to be thrown, not to be put off, by a varied guidance on the part of the Holy Spirit.

Take, for example, the fact that he was led *by the circumstance of persecution* to leave Jerusalem and go to Samaria. That is, the Spirit employed the pressure of persecution to lead him out from Jerusalem and out from the mother church there to the wider ministry that was to be his in Samaria and elsewhere. So we read, in verse 1 of chapter 8, "On that day a great persecution arose against the church in Jerusalem; and they were all scattered throughout the region of Judea and Samaria, except the apostles—"that is the Twelve. And then in verse 4: "Now those who were scattered went about preaching the word. Philip"—for one—"went down to a city of Samaria." Here is the Spirit guiding through circumstances—in this case the circumstance of opposition.

Or again, Philip was led *by the ministry of an angel.* Look at verse 26. Right in the midst of this immensely successful mission we read, "But an angel of the Lord said to Philip, 'Rise and go toward the south to the road that goes down from Jerusalem to Gaza.'" The ministry of an angel! An extraordinary thing! Do you believe in angels? I hope you do. Many people are so sophisticated these days that they don't believe in angels. They want us to believe that all that went out of the window with spooks and the rest! But if you and I are going to take the Bible seriously, I think we are bound to believe in angels. The invisible realm is peopled with intelligences—some of whom are fallen and therefore in conspiracy with Satan—but multitudes of whom are the servants of the Lord God Almighty, and probably have much more to do with our lives than most of us realize. Philip was led by the special ministry of an angel.

Or again, verse 29, Philip was led *by an inner voice,* the direct, subjective voice of the Holy Spirit. "And the Spirit said to Philip, 'Go up and join this chariot.' So Philip ran to him." The inner speaking of the Holy Spirit!

Now someone who is reading is saying, "I'm glad he has got to this. I am troubled and confused about it. How do I recognize, how do I identify, the voice of the Spirit? I seem to hear various voices speaking. How do I know which is the Holy Spirit?" Well, for one thing, the Holy Spirit speaking within your consciousness, will never lead you to do anything contrary to the plain, revealed, recorded teachings of Jesus. That is one way you may know. If the inner voice tells you to do some foolish thing, or some wrong thing in violation of the plain teaching of the Word of God, you know it is not the Spirit who is speaking. This is why we are to "try the spirits" to see whether or not it is really the voice of the Holy Spirit speaking.

Furthermore, the Spirit never leads you to run away from some obviously urgent duty. To be sure, sometimes your relatives or friends try to make you feel you have got a duty. That's another matter. I refer to plain, undeniable duty. Let me recall for you an incident of which I once read from the life of Gipsy Smith. A lady came to him and said, "I feel called to preach."

The dear Gipsy evidently suspected something was wrong, so he began to ask her some questions. He said, "How old are you?"

To the query about her age she replied, as I remember it, "I am forty-five."

"Have you any children?"

"Oh, yes, I have ten." In response to his question about their ages she gave him facts, right up the ladder. Some of them were not yet in their teens.

He said, "My dear lady, I have no doubt in the world that you are called to preach and the Lord has given you your congregation. Stick to it!"

No, the Spirit is not going to tell you to do something that leads you to run away from obvious duty.

Another thing. Some of you, though you know all this, are confused at times. Even the more mature Christians among us will tell you, quite honestly, that it isn't *always* easy for them to detect the voice of the Spirit within. Therefore, let me suggest that if you miss it once in a while, you are not to be discouraged and disillusioned. You are not to say, "Oh, there's nothing in this talk about living a guided life." No! Remember that the Holy Spirit almost never speaks hurriedly and agitatedly to you. His is a quiet voice. It is a gentle voice. And with practice—*with practice*—you'll learn to detect it, at least in most instances, without much difficulty.

Now if this appears to have been something of a digression, I hope it has been a profitable one. The point is that here, in the case of Philip, we have a man who was flexibly in touch with the Holy Spirit. Philip didn't say, "Well now, the *last* time God guided me an angel came. I've got to have an angel *this* time!" Just the gentle inner speaking of the Holy Spirit was enough. Or Philip was not among those who say, "Well, the Lord really spoke to me the other time. I don't hear any voice *now*." He recognized the pressure of circumstances, as being a form of guidance. Flexibly in touch with the Holy Spirit!

Second, we find that Philip was not only pliable as to how he should be led by the Spirit, he was flexible *as to where he should be used by the Spirit*. Try to imagine Philip's situation. Here in Samaria immense success! The whole city stirred! Masses of people turning to Christ! Great joy filling the city!

There was even a man there by the name of Simon

Magus, a notorious magician, who had been the idol of the people. So powerful was the work of the Holy Spirit through Philip that Simon Magus lost his crowd, forfeited his following. He was terribly perturbed by it. For once, at least, people preferred an evangelist to an enchanter, a soul-winner to a sorcerer. But now suddenly, in the midst of this thrilling mission, the Lord leads him away. Where? Of all places, to the desert! Look at verses 26-29 in chapter 8. "But an angel of the Lord said to Philip, 'Rise and go toward the south to the road that goes down from Jerusalem to Gaza.' This is a desert road. And he rose and went. And behold, an Ethiopian, a eunuch, a minister of Candace the queen of the Ethiopians, in charge of all her treasure, had come to Jerusalem to worship and was returning; seated in his chariot, he was reading the prophet Isaiah. And the Spirit said to Philip, 'Go up and join this chariot.' " From a teeming city to a lonely desert! From a place where he was ministering to multitudes to a place where he had a congregation of one—an Ethiopian eunuch!

Do you believe that God wants people who are flexible like this? I do. Please, I beg of you, if God has done some great thing through you, something that perhaps has been taken notice of by many people and written up in the press, don't be so big and important that you cannot serve Him joyously in some little sphere or in dealing with only one person. Do something gracefully and joyously that will never be written up in the papers—something that so far from being ignored by The *Times* or The *Tribune* will not even appear in *The Life of Faith.* (And if you think my comparison belittles *The Life of Faith,* I can only give you my personal assurance that I wish *The Life of Faith* had as big a circulation as the *New York Times*).

Oh, for people in our churches who are flexible as to where God wants to use them! A missionary said to me in India a few months ago, when we were talking about our mutual friend, Billy Graham, "You know, I was in Toronto on furlough and Billy was having a tremendous campaign, with throngs waiting on his ministry. I had a problem at that time in my life, and I did so much want to see him, but it was difficult for anybody to get to him because of the demands on his time." "But," he went on, "as it turned out, I was right at one of the exits when Billy was going out with some of his colleagues. He spied me and, calling me by my first name, he said, 'Come with me and let's talk a few moments.'" The missionary continued: "We went to his hotel and had a quiet talk together." He then remarked to me that Billy would never know how much that little incident meant to him. The value of it lay not only in the counsel Dr. Graham gave but also, and quite as much, in the act itself—the turning aside from a thronged auditorium for one lonely and perplexed missionary. Flexible as to *where* we are to be used!

b) Come now for a second look at Philip as he appears in the noonday light of his ministry. If he was flexibly in touch with the Spirit, he was *firmly in touch with the gospel*. Notwithstanding the fact that he was not a theologian like Paul nor an apostle like Peter, he was nonetheless in firm and faithful possession of the essential content of the gospel. I want you to see how many phrases are used to describe this priceless thing with which all of us have been put in trust, whether we are laymen or ministers. In verse 4 there is the phrase, "the word: . . . those who were scattered went about preaching the word." In verse 5 there is the phrase (in the RSV) "the Christ": Philip went down to a city in Samaria, and proclaimed to them the Christ. In verse 12, the phrase is "good news": ". . . when they believed Philip as he preached the good news. . . ." That, of course, is what the word "gospel" literally means. There is another phrase in verse 12, "the name of Jesus Christ": "the good news about the Kingdom of God and the name of Jesus Christ." Some of these phrases are repeated as the narrative goes on. For example, we read in verse 35, ". . . Philip opened his mouth, and beginning with this scripture he told him the good news of Jesus." Again, and finally, in verse 40, ". . . Philip was found at Azotus, and passing on he preached the gospel to all the towns till he came to Caesarea."

Now whatever the phrasing—"the word," "the Christ," "the name," the "good news"—it has to do with one central thing into the meaning of which Philip has personally entered and in the proclamation of which he spoke with persuasive conviction. The gospel, you see, is not what men think about God, or what men strive to do to make themselves acceptable to God. That is religion, but it is not the gospel. The gospel is what *God* has done. It is His breaking into history and into time with His virgin-born Son, and taking your sins and mine and making an atonement for them by the blood of His cross, then sealing that victory over sin and death and the devil by His mighty resurrection. Those who receive the message find that their believing reception of it is the open door into new life. They become part of a new community, the community of the redeemed, who in turn are expected to proclaim the good news to others. To have a firm hold on all of this, and to feel responsibility for the sharing of it with others, is to stand in the splendid tradition of this man Philip. Such people are enormously needed.

c) There is one more thing to be said of this man in the noontime of his power and influence: he was *fondly in touch with people.* If it had not been so, if he had not loved people with an affection that was Christ's own gift to him, do you think he would have gone where he did go? He went to Samaria. Recall what the woman of Samaria said to Jesus when He opened conversation with her: "How is it that you, a Jew, ask a drink of me, a woman of Samaria?" Samaritans were a mongrel race. The Jews despised them. The Samaritans resented it. Nevertheless, it was to a "city of Samaria" that Philip went, according to verse 5, ". . . and proclaimed to them the Christ." Or take the case of the Ethiopian. He was a Gentile. The point is that Philip loved people just because they were people—for whom Christ died. Calvary love had stripped him of racial haughtiness and hostility.

There was a Christian woman several years ago who was riding in what—before the Civil Rights Act—we called a Jim Crow car on the railway—part of it for Negroes only and part for whites only. The Negro section was full so when the train made a stop and an elderly Negro attempted to get on, the guard said, "No, you can't ride; we are full."

He said, "My son is dying and I've got to go!"

Overhearing this, the lady spoke up: "Allow him to sit here by me."

The guard looked at her, startled, and said; "Do you mean that?"

She said, "I mean it," so he was permitted to travel. As they rode along she conversed with him.

When he left the train, the lady sitting behind her said, "How could you do that?"

She said, "Do what?"

"Oh, have that colored man sit beside you, and talk to him as you did."

"Why" she said, "that's easy to answer. I could do it because I serve a Master who is color-blind!"

A delightful answer, wasn't it? Philip, I think, would have loved it. St. Paul would have agreed with it. He was sure that in Christ "the middle wall of partition," or, as the RSV has it, "the dividing wall of hostility" (Ephesians 2:14), has been broken down.

Flexibly in touch with the Holy Spirit, firmly in touch with the gospel, and fondly in touch with people —that was this greatheart of the early church.

III

THE TWILIGHT

In the final glimpse of Philip that the record allows us to have we see a thrilling career drawing to a quiet close. As nearly as New Testament scholars can calculate, an interval of about twenty years lies between the time of Philip's Samaritan ministry and his receiving St.

Paul as a guest in his home in Caesarea: "On the morrow we departed and came to Caesarea; and we entered the house of Philip the evangelist, who was one of the seven, and stayed with him. And he had four unmarried daughters, who prophesied" (21:8, 9).

Between Acts 8 and Acts 21, two decades! How long was Philip engaged in such large-scale action as that which we have seen in Samaria? We do not know. How long did he continue to be a roving evangelist, as St. Paul was? History is silent on the point. The one thing that seems clear is that when we meet him again, in Acts 21, he is exercising an unspectacular ministry—one that was perhaps confined largely to his own place of residence—in Caesarea. Indeed more noteworthy than any prophesying that Philip may have been doing at this time was the fact that his four daughters were known for their prophetic gifts. And this in the world of the East, which is a *man's* world!

The big meetings are over. The huge throngs are no more. The lilt and lift of the sensational went with the yesterdays. The glare of noonday softened into the mellowness of twilight!

The art of growing old gracefully is best learned in the school of Christ. The capacity for an unembittered lapse into obscurity, never easy to come by, is best acquired "beneath the Cross of Jesus." Dr. W. E. Sangster, in his Westminster Series pamphlet on *How to Live in Christ,* has a brief section that he calls "As the Shadows Lengthen." It is addressed to those for whom the mounting years have slackened the pace of life. In a haunting phrase he speaks of those who experience "the hurt of waning powers." How much or how little of

71

this hurt Philip had felt, one cannot say. In any case the record holds no hint that his spirit had grown rancid with cynicism or gray with disenchantment. Far from his fading into futility, as might have been the case, Philip simply faded into a serene victory.

I like to remember, for example, that while *he faded from prominence, he did not fade from obedience.* Demas faded—shabbily, tragically. He forsook Paul. He forsook the Lord. His was the defeat of a disloyal soul. Not Philip! The obedience that took him from Jerusalem to Samaria, from Samaria to the desert, from the desert to a princely chariot, was still his holy habit when last we have a look at him. Let our popularity with *others* pass if only our loyalty to *Him* remains.

And then I like to remember that while *Philip faded from fame, he did not fade from fruitfulness.* There were those "four unmarried daughters who prophesied." Instead of being frustrated and peevish maidens, they were radiant and articulate spinsters. A happy harvest from fine parental sowing! What lightning calculator could furnish a sudden tally of the tears and the prayers and the myriad impingements of persuasive example that had gone into the making of these gifted ladies. "They still bring fruit in old age," cried the psalmist, 'they are ever full of sap and green." Philip's twilight years gave proof that the psalmist was right.

I like to think, finally, that while *this man faded from the ministry of signs, he did not fade from the ministry of saintliness.* Here in this quiet Caesarean home, "far from the madding crowd," the man who once served tables was himself being served by those who loved him, and the man who once traveled to points remote and risky now bore his witness mostly, it would appear, within the constricted orbit of his own home. Sharp—perhaps sometimes tempting—were the contrasts between the past and now. ". . . the multitudes with one accord gave heed to what was said by Philip, when they heard him and saw the signs which he did" (8:6). Where were the signs now? Gone—at least so far as the record runs. Big crowds, big miracles, big tumult—all gone.

Yet something bigger than signs remains: that character aura of Christlikeness which is the hallmark of the saint. It's a beauty that banishes bitterness, a sweetness that surmounts sourness, a tranquility that triumphs over turbulence. The mark of a saint is that when career glamor is utterly gone, character glow shines on.

Thomas Carlyle said of De Quincy that he was "full of bankrupt enthusiasms." No such ashen emptiness will you find in the heart of a saint. The Moffatt translation has St. Paul saying to the Roman Christians, "Maintain the spiritual glow."

Philip did—to the end.

No, it was Christ in him who did!

5 *Paul:*

The Man Who Kept the Vision

TEXT: ". . . I was not disobedient to the heavenly vision. . . ." Acts 26:19.

IN THE 26TH Chapter of the Acts, we have the word that Paul gave by way of witness before a pagan king, King Agrippa; here he reviews his life—partly before his conversion to Christ, but for the most part afterwards. And he says, beginning with verse 9: "I myself was convinced that I ought to do many things in opposing the name of Jesus of Nazareth. And I did so in Jerusalem; I not only shut up many of the saints in prison, by authority from the chief priests, but when they were put to death I cast my vote against them. And I punished them often in all the synagogues and tried to make them blaspheme; I tried to make those Christians blaspheme; and in raging fury against them, I persecuted them even to foreign cities.

75

"Thus I journeyed to Damascus"—about 150 miles away up in the north country from Jerusalem—"with the authority and commission of the chief priests. At midday, O king, I saw on the way a light from heaven, brighter than the sun, shining round me and those who journeyed with me. And when we had all fallen to the ground, I heard a voice saying to me in the Hebrew language, 'Saul, Saul, why do you persecute me? It hurts you to kick against the goads.' And I said, 'Who are you, Lord?' And the Lord said, 'I am Jesus whom you are persecuting. But rise and stand upon your feet; for I have appeared to you for this purpose, to appoint you to serve and bear witness to the things in which you have seen me and to those in which I will appear to you, delivering you from the people—that is, the Jews—and from the Gentiles—to whom I send you to open their eyes, that they may turn from darkness to light and from the power of Satan to God, that they may receive forgiveness of sins and a place among those who are sanctified by faith in me.'

"Wherefore, O King Agrippa, I was not disobedient to the heavenly vision, but declared first to those at Damascus, then at Jerusalem and throughout all the country of Judea, and also to the Gentiles, that they should repent and turn to God and perform deeds worthy of their repentance. For this reason the Jews seized me in the temple and tried to kill me. To this day"—think now of the span of years between then and his conversion—"I have had the help that comes from God, and so I stand here testifying both to small and great, saying nothing but what the prophets and Moses said would come to pass: that the Christ must suffer, and that, by being the first to rise from the dead, he would proclaim light both to the people and to the Gentiles."

Now you may have guessed from the chapter title, "Paul, the Man Who Kept the Vision," what our key verse is. It is verse 19, "Wherefore, O King Agrippa, I was not disobedient to the heavenly vision." Vision is used, as you know, in more than one way in our English language. If an optometrist or an oculist says to you, "You have 20-20 vision," he means that your vision is normal; you are very thankful that he does say this particular thing. But people can have 20-20 vision and go through life tragically blind. Paul was doing that before he found Christ. There is a tradition that Paul had bad eyesight from the time of his conversion; some believe this eye difficulty was related to the blinding light that smote him. In any case, I simply want to point out to you that sight—physical sight—is one thing and insight is another. Paul became a man of insight with respect to Jesus Christ, and the Christian gospel, and the Christian faith, and the purposes of God in this world and for eternity.

Now just a thumbnail sketch of Paul's life: He was a Hellenistic Jew; he was not born in Palestine. His parents were ardent Jews, but he was born to them in the city of Tarsus in Cilicia, a province of Rome. He was taught, in due course, as every Jewish boy was taught, some form of manual craft, which probably accounts for his knowing how to make tents. I say this because sometimes it is suggested that Paul could not have been a first-class scholar and of the aristocracy if he learned a humble craft like tent-making. Nothing strange about it at all! This was a common practice, and not a bad one either. No matter who he was, from a family of the rich or the learned class, he must have some manual skill.

However, young Saul was indeed an aristrocrat, socially, intellectually, and religiously. At fifteen, he began his training to become a rabbi, and he sat at the feet of one of the most famous, one of the most liberal-minded and large-hearted, of the rabbis of that day—Gamaliel. From a Greek city where he had absorbed Greek philosophy and Greek culture, to a famous Jewish rabbi where he became steeped in the laws and the traditions of the Jews!

Then came an episode in his life from which he never recovered. It was the martyrdom of Stephen. Saul could never get away from the way Stephen died, that light in Stephen's face, that complete absence of resentment or retaliation in Stephen's heart, his dying, like his Lord, praying for his murderers, "Lord, lay not this sin to their charge."

And then something happened to Paul that sometimes happens in some degree, to a lot of people whom you and I have met.

In my years as a minister—and especially those years when I was spending full time in evangelism—I have had people get very very upset with the evangelist, and even rude to him. Why? Because they disliked *him?* No; that was only a smoke screen. It was because they were inwardly convicted of *sin*, and they were taking it out on somebody! There is a psychological mechanism, with which psychiatrists are well acquainted, called overcompensation. In your heart is a terrible conflict. You know

78

there is a certain course of action you really ought to take, but you are not prepared to take it, and so, to compensate for your unwillingness, you develop an obsessive and rationalizing pattern of reaction to this thing. Saul became infuriated against the Christians. He said, "They have got to go, and the cause has got to die, and the name of Jesus has got to be forgotten."

So for a time he gave himself with abandon to this frightful, this murderous, hostility against the Christians and the Christian faith. And on this particular day, having vented his rage around Jerusalem and having heard that there were Christians away up in Damascus, he was armed with authority from the chief priests to go up to this Syrian city to deal with the Christians there and get rid of them. You can know how madly zealous he was because he puts a little touch into the story that is significant. He says, "at midday." At midday! There he was, traveling eagerly, recklessly, murder in his heart, at midday. "Well," you say, "there is nothing strange about that, is there?" There is indeed, because in that part of the world under the fierce sun you didn't travel at midday. You took a siesta. But Saul was so bent on his murderous errand that he didn't even stop to rest a bit in the middle of the day. On with the job! Ah, little did he dream, five minutes before this event took place, what was about to happen.

The light broke! *The light broke!* Some people think it was a thunderstorm and that Saul was stunned with lightning. I was stunned with lightning once, when I was a boy. It was a dreadful experience. It wasn't a direct hit, or I wouldn't be alive to tell about it; but the bolt went off so close that I was stunned by it. Even

now, after all these years— I was then a lad of seven—
I can still remember the blinding flash and then my
being paralyzed for the moment.

I doubt that this was Paul's experience. I think it rather
profitless to try to determine the exact and precise *form*
of this vision so far as its external features were concerned. It was far too objective to be an hallucination.
Forever thereafter it stood in Paul's mind as a revelation of the risen Jesus.

You know what followed. Temporarily he was blinded.
What to do? To be sure, he had orders from the chief
priests, but suddenly they were useless. Little did they
realize that something had happened to Saul that would
prevent his taking orders from them any more.

He began to take orders from Jesus. "Who are you,
Lord?"

"I am Jesus whom thou persecutest." "You can't touch
one of mine without touching Me," said Jesus in effect.
"I am Jesus! Rise and go into the city, and there is a
man there who will take you the rest of the way into
the new life I have for you."

He met that dear man, Ananias, who told him the
good news of the crucified and risen Messiah. He prayed
with him. He saw a new faith spring to birth in Saul's
heart. The scales of his unbelief fell from his eager eyes.
Baptism was administered. And thus began what is without any shadow of doubt the greatest career in 1900
years of church history.

You can characterize many Bible figures by a phrase,
by singling out something that is prominent and domi-
nant. You can't do that with Paul. What Socrates is to
philosophy, and Shakespeare is to literature, St. Paul is

to the Christian faith and the Christian church. There was a manifoldness, a totalness, about Paul that is quite staggering.

For a little time he tried to give his witness in Damascus. Then the Jews turned on him. This occasioned the quiet interlude—about two years, some say three—in Arabia, for a deeper revelation of Christ to him—" . . . to reveal his Son in me . . . ," as Paul puts it in Galatians; and then from seven to eight years when he is back in Tarsus, and nobody hears anything about him. Then Barnabas, because of the magnitude of the work of the gospel in Antioch, goes over to Tarsus to fetch Paul. And now the incredibly active and adventurous career is launched on its way: the first missionary journey which lasted three years; the second missionary journey, which lasted about three years—two whole years of that time in one city alone, the city of Ephesus; then the third missionary journey, covering perhaps two years; and then the beginning of the end.

Persecution is closing in on him. He appeals to Caesar for that justice of which Rome was proud. For two years he is a prisoner in Caesarea. He is removed to Rome, and shipwrecked in the process. There are two more years of imprisonment in the imperial city.

And now the Book of Acts closes and tradition moves in. What remains of the story is not part of the inspired New Testament record. It is just a moderately respectable tradition which has in it, I must say, much that appeals to us. Paul was released from that first imprisonment in Rome. This gave him his opportunity to carry out his fond wish to preach the gospel in Spain. When he came back, there was a new Caesar—Nero. Nero was blaming the Christians for everything that went wrong in Rome. If, for example, a fire broke out, the Christians had started it.

Nero went off on a trip while Paul was there. The tradition says that one of his many mistresses, one of his favorites indeed, was won to the Saviour by St. Paul. When Nero got home, his concubine was gone. She had joined the Christian group as a follower of the Lord Jesus. Nero was so infuriated that he began wreaking his vengeance on Paul. The apostle's second Roman imprisonment was brief. They took him out the Ostian Way to a spot where you may have stood, and severed his head from his body. But it was with Paul as Dwight L. Moody said it would be one day with him. Once, when he was preaching, Mr. Moody exclaimed, "One of these days you are going to hear that Dwight L. Moody is dead. Don't believe a word of it! For he will be more alive *then* than he has ever been in his life." So to behead Paul was not to destroy him; it was to release him into everlasting vitality and honor and influence.

I

LIFE'S DELIVERER

Let us consider now, more explicitly, this vision that Paul kept so steadfastly and so splendidly. First of all, there was the *Vision of Life's Deliverer*, and Paul kept that to the end. You notice in verse 17 that Paul recalls the revolutionary and reassuring word Christ spoke to him, " . . . delivering you from the people and from the Gentiles . . ." Now somehow this word "deliver," became a tremendous word with Paul. You can't have deliverance without a deliverer; and the deliverer was the Lord who had now captured him.

Let us turn for a quick moment to Colossians 1:13: "He"—that is, the Father-God—"has delivered us from the dominion of darkness and transferred us to the kingdom of his beloved Son." There is *deliverance from sin's tyranny*, with the dominion of darkness broken and the kingdom of light ushered in. God's beloved Son has done it.

Or look at Galatians 1:3-4. Right here in the beginning of the Galatian letter, Paul says, "Grace to you and peace from God the Father and our Lord Jesus Christ, who gave himself for our sins to deliver us from the present evil age." Here is *deliverance from the world's tentacles*. It is essentially godless. There is a vast complex of evil that surrounds us. It is essentially godless because it lives in disregard of God's kingdom, laws, and love. Its heart is set on the perishable. Its ego is the center of its life. It grips us like a vice. It shapes us, dictates to us, dominates us—until Christ sets us free. How many people there are who don't mold their environment, but are molded by it! That's why Paul says, in Phillips' translation of Romans 12:2, "Don't let the world . . . squeeze you into its own mold. . . ." This translation hits straight home, for that is what the world is always trying to do. But Christ delivers us, says St. Paul; He makes us free from the world's grip, from the clutching grasp of a world system that has its deadly hold upon people who are unchanged and unreleased by the gospel.

Or look at I Thessalonians 1:9-10. At the end of this

chapter in which Paul has been reviewing the remarkable way in which the transforming gospel of the Son of God came to these Thessalonians, he says, " . . . you turned to God from idols, to serve a living and true God, and to wait for his Son from heaven"—notice now!— "whom he raised from the dead, Jesus who delivers us from the wrath to come." Deliverance from sin's tyranny? Yes. Deliverance from the world's tentacles? Yes. And *deliverance*—thank God—*from judgment's terror*. He has delivered us from "the wrath to come." Jesus, you remember, said, "He who believes in him is not condemned; he who does not believe is condemned already, because he has not believed in the name of the only Son of God" (John 3:18). This was the vision—the vision of the Supreme Deliverer, that came to Paul, and from which he never departed wherever he went. It was in the light of this vision that he proclaimed, with such passionate persuasiveness, the unsearchable riches of Jesus Christ.

II

LIFE'S DESIGN

Second, there was the *Vision of Life's Design*, and Paul kept that with immovable steadfastness. In verse 16 there is an expression that provides us with our clue in respect to this point. Please notice: " . . . rise and stand upon your feet; for I have appeared unto you for this purpose. . . ." Life in Christ is invariably life with a purpose. One of the great tragedies of our day is the sheer aimlessness, purposelessness, of so many young

84

people. Nor are they all under privileged boys: they may be university students.

My friend, Dr. Louis Evans, while he was still pastor of the great First Presbyterian Church in Hollywood, California, was asked to come over to a bull session—a free-and-easy discussion in one of the fraternity houses. There were about thirty men in this fraternity sitting around on the floor. When Dr. Evans was introduced he said, "Now if you don't mind, I'd like to go 'round the circle, getting your answer to one question: What is the purpose of my life?" He said the very first boy who answered said, "I plan to be a pharmacist."

Dr. Evans said, "Oh, apparently I haven't made my question clear. If you are going into pharmacy, that means that by pharmacy you are going to make your living. That isn't what I am asking. What is the purpose of your *life?*"

Many people are confused at that point. Between making a living and making a life there is a world of difference. Dr. Evans said they went 'round the circle, and out of thirty university men, only three—incidentally this first one dropped his head and said, "Well, I'm sorry, but I haven't thought that one through"—only three could make any respectably intelligent statement about the real purpose, the fundamental design, of life.

All this to the contrary, when you are captured by Jesus Christ, as Paul was that day on the Damascus road, you may be sure that God has a design for you. He gives to your life a meaning and a goal. This basic purpose has nothing to do with whether you are a nurse or a doctor or an engineer or an accountant or a farmer or an airline captain. These jobs are the means by which

85

we keep body and soul together. Yet there is something that makes these jobs more than secular. What is it? What is it that lifts them and transfigures them into something authentically spiritual? It is the higher purpose of life that invades and informs and irradiates our daily job, making it, as an affair of bread-and-butter, secondary to the overriding aim of bearing witness to Jesus Christ and to those "things," those saving realities, in which He has appeared to us.

Away with this popular fancy that spirituality consists only of saying prayers, or singing hymns, or reading the Bible! "I am serving Christ," wrote David Livingstone, "when shooting a buffalo for my men, or taking an astronomical observation, or writing to one of His children who forget." That strikes the right note—the note of purpose and mission threading its meaningful way through all that we do.

If now, more specifically, we ask, "What are these 'things' of Christian faith and experience for witness to which we have been given our discipleship?" then the answer is ready at hand in what Paul heard from the Lord on the day of his conversion. He hears the risen Jesus say, " . . . to open their eyes, that they may turn from darkness to light and from the power of Satan to God, that they may receive forgiveness of sins and a place among those who are sanctified by faith in me" (Acts 26: 18-19). Analyze this. See how lofty and luminous is the purpose of Christ for His church and for you as a redeemed member of it.

He expects from us *a witness that strikes home as light:* "to open their eyes." It was so with Paul; it is so with us. "The issue of our day," says Trevor Huddleston, famed author of *Nought for Your Comfort,* "is the issue of communicating to a pagan, post-Christian world: a world that has heard a language and relegated it to the four walls of a church; a world which will only hear that language again if it can come with a freshness, a stimulus, a shining sparkle." If that witness is given, there will be those, in numbers great or small, whose eyes will be opened to the false values of the life they are living, and to the burden and boredom of the sins of which they are guilty, and to the glory of the Christ to whom they have been so incredibly blind.

Christ expects from us, moreover, *a witness that is creative of repentance:* "that they may turn from darkness to light and from the power of Satan to God." In his helpful little book called *Basic Christianity,* John Stott has a paragraph on repentance in which he says, "Repentance is a definite turning from every thought, word, deed, and habit which is known to be wrong. It is not sufficient to feel pangs of remorse or to make some kind of apology to God. Fundamentally, repentance is a matter neither of emotion nor speech. It is an inward change of mind and attitude towards sin which leads to a change of behavior."

They who are indeed Christ's disciples have been through this; and, having been through it, they live daily in the *spirit* of forgiven penitents, and thus are used to bring the call to repentance straight home to those who remain complacent about their sins.

Again, Christ expects from us *a witness that speaks of pardon:* "that they may receive forgiveness of sins." "In the person of his Son," cries Karl Barth, "God suffers his own judgment against sin. He is at once judge and

87

judged. And it is thus that sin is blotted out radically, efficaciously." It is this towering fact that gives us the gospel. To be Christ's man or woman is to have proved it; and, proving it for oneself, one bears witness to it before others.

> Pardon—from an offended God!
> Pardon—for sins of deepest dye!
> Pardon—bestowed through Jesus' blood!
> Pardon—that brings the rebel nigh!
>
> Who is a pardoning God like Thee?
> Or who has grace so rich and free?

Finally, Christ expects from us *a witness that points to sanctity:* "and a place among those who are sanctified by faith in me." Professor William Barclay is of the opinion that in the New Testament the basic idea of the word "holy" is "different." As, for example, the Sabbath Day is holy because it is different from other days, so the Christian is holy because he is different from other persons. This may be useful as a starting point for discussion, but it scarcely does more. Of what does the difference consist?

A Christian is holy *positionally*, let us say, because he is in Christ and Christ is in him. This is our *common* sanctification as believers.

A Christian is, or should be, hol*y penetratively* because he has in fact begun to accept the implications of holy obedience to a holy Lord and to claim, by faith, that power of the cross by which the self-mind is canceled out in submission to the Christ-mind. This is our *crucial* sanctification. "The very God of peace sanctify you wholly." The tense of the verb is the Greek *aorist*—something done, settled.

And then, also, a Christian is holy *progressively* because the pure heart is not the same as the mature character. The earnest Christian life is a perpetual paradox of gift and growth, of arrival and non-arrival, of perfection and imperfection: a gift of radical cleansing and a growth in radiant Christlikeness, an arrival at the principle of deadness to sin and a non-arrival at complacency over rebukes from the Holy Spirit, a perfection in love and an imperfection in service. I have read that before Columbus dared the Atlantic and discovered America, maps of Europe showed Gibraltar and just beyond it the Latin words *Ne Plus Ultra*—"nothing beyond." After America's discovery it was suggested that the *ne* should be erased, leaving *Plus Ultra*—"everything beyond." So with the Christian: no Gibraltar of crisis-sanctification must ever give rise to the fancy that now it is *Ne Plus Ultra*. Crisis-sanctification must be blended with process-sanctification in which there is always more, much, everything, beyond.

St. Paul found all of this in his own experience of Christ. He found it all to be a part of God's design for his life. And he shared it all with unflinching fidelity. He was true to the vision of life's design.

III

LIFE'S DESTINY

And then finally, there was the *Vision of Life's Destiny*, and Paul was true to that. Look at verse 23. From the beginning, says Paul to Agrippa, my mission was to testify "that the Christ must suffer, and that, by being the first to rise from the dead, he would proclaim light both to the people and to the Gentiles." What we want is to seize upon this very significant reference to the resurrection of the Lord Jesus. For Paul found in that resurrection the pledge, indeed not only the pledge but the pattern, both of his own resurrection in the end, and the resurrection of God's own people. Thus you hear him say, for example, " . . . our commonwealth is in heaven, and from it we await a Savior, the Lord Jesus Christ, who will change our lowly body to be like his glorious body, by the power which enables him even to subject all things to himself" (Philippians 3:20).

Paul's vision flashes light on *the grim subject of death*. Death is conquered through the resurrection of Jesus, and they who are "in Christ," though they die, will rise again.

Paul's vision flashes light on *the glowing subject of Christ's return;* "we await a Savior."

Paul's vision flashes light on *the glorious subject of the soul's long home*. When it came to the end he said, "I have finished the course. I have kept the faith." That by way of review.

And *this* by way of *prospect:* " . . . the time of my departure is at hand." Departure! It is the word that Jesus used on the Mount of Transfiguration. He spoke to Moses and Elias concerning His "decease," His going out, His exodus, His departure. And in our case, in St. Paul's case, in your case, it is going home. Christians are pilgrims, but thank God they are not tramps! The difference between a pilgrim and a tramp is that a tramp goes in circles, he doesn't know where he is going, and doesn't particularly care; but a pilgrim has his eye on the home goal.

When my father, at seventy-nine, having preached Christ for sixty years, was dying in Pasadena, California, a five-o'clock dawn was spreading beautifully over our Sierra Madre Mountains. He was conscious almost to the last. Because I saw he was trying to say something to me, I bent over him and said, "What did you say, father?"

The faintest smile came over his face as he whispered, "I'm almost home!" Like our gallant St. Paul, he had not been "disobedient to the heavenly vision."

The vision of life's deliverer: without Christ life is useless.

The vision of life's design: without Christ life is aimless.

The vision of life's destiny: without Christ life is hopeless.

6 *Mark:*

The Man Who Came Back

TEXT: *"...Get Mark, and bring him with you: for he is very useful in serving me."*
—*II Timothy 4:11.*

SOMEONE—GLADSTONE *I* believe it was—made the remark that if we want an antidote for the poison of discouragement, we should read biographies. In the way others have triumphed over their troubles we find a clue to our own conquests. This is particularly true of many of the lives that are sketched for us in the Bible.

Take, for example, the case of this man Mark. The New Testament account of him is brief. It can be gathered up in about a dozen scattered verses. Yet those verses are packed with drama, with pathos, with failure, with success: in a word, with all the vividly contrasting colors of sin and grace. Here is the career of a man who started well, failed pathetically, then succeeded splen-

93

didly. It is a story not without warning, but rich nevertheless in encouragement. A man *can* come back!

To begin with, however, we must know something about his failure.

I

Here was a man who *beat a retreat.*

His first commission is an honorable one. Paul and Barnabas are about to set out on their first missionary journey. They need a helper, a kind of personal attendant who would at the same time be able to give some instruction to the new converts to the Christian faith. Barnabas, Mark's uncle, suggests to Paul that the young man would make an excellent companion. It is agreed. Comes the day of departure, and John Mark, thrilled no doubt that he can fare forth in such noble company, sets out high-heartedly upon the great adventure. Thus we read, "So, being sent out by the Holy Spirit, they went down to Seleucia, and from there they sailed to Cyprus . . . and they had also John (Mark) to assist them" (Acts 13.4,5).

All went well for a time. "I love this," thought Mark, as they made their way to the coast and set sail for the island of Cyprus. "New faces to see, new cities to visit, new territory to claim for Christ, new experiences to report to the folks back home!" Novelty usually has its fascinations, and Mark was not indifferent to them. True, even Cyprus was a long way from home for a young man making his first trip into new lands. And then this business of associating so much with Gentiles, trying to persuade them that they were as much the object of

Christ's love and redeeming grace as the Jews, well, to say the least, that was new and strange and not altogether to Mark's taste.

Something else troubled Mark. It was that strange, faraway look in Paul's eyes. It was that plan he heard Paul and Barnabas discussing: they were actually proposing to travel much farther from the home base. In fact they were getting ready to sail for the mainland of Asia Minor, and invade that wild country with its unbridged rivers and its dangerous mountain passes and its barbarous people. This man Paul! Why does he burn with such passionate fondness for these pagans? Why is he so restless, so determined, so burdened, to get on to the next town and preach there? Why can he never be satisfied with what he has already done? Why not try to conserve the results already won?

And so John Mark began to "rationalize" his inner collapse. He lacked the power to see things through. Vaguely he realized it, but, like most of us, he reached desperately for some excuse to cover his failure.

Then came the crisis. Night falls over the blue Mediterranean. Paul sleeps. Barnabas sleeps. But not Mark. No Hamlet, holding tense council with himself, and murmuring confusedly,

> To be, or not to be,
> That is the question,

ever presented a more dramatic picture than I fancy John Mark did, as he walked alone that night, wrestling with the issue of going on or turning back. "To be or not to be!" To be a plodder, or to be a quitter! To be a coward, or to be a hero! To be loyal to myself, my co-workers, my Christ, or to let them all down! That was the question. That was the battle.

The night wears on. "I can't go any farther," says Mark inwardly.

"But I went farther," says Christ. "I went to Calvary for you—and for these Gentiles as well."

And then a third voice speaks. It is the bewitching voice of the Devil, thrown, by a strange ventriloquy, out of the very depths of hell. "Get away from it all"— so the voice whispers, huskily, insinuatingly. "You were excited when you started anyhow. Just quietly chuck the whole thing—this business of taking Christ seriously and going out to live and work for Him. You'll have it a lot easier back home. If you want to go to the synagogue occasionally, all right; but there's no use giving up so much 'for Jesus,' as they say, or for some brave ideal of service, or for some fancied reward in the 'Sweet Bye and Bye.'"

Silence now. It is deep in the night. The battle is over—for the moment at least. Decision has been made. The morning dawns. Paul and Barnabas are ready to continue their journey. But where is John Mark? He is gone!

Mark, at daybreak, is in full retreat, leaving his older companions to carry on for Christ without him. Look him over, I beseech you, and see if you do not recognize yourself. You too started out with the Master, sincere in your faith, enthusiastic in your devotion. You too had a vision of doing worth while things for Jesus Christ, that the borders of His Kingdom might be broadened. You too found yourself up against unexpected difficulties, with a stiff price to pay for your faith and a long, gray road of unrewarding toil to travel. And you too lost your nerve. You too gave up when the going got heavy and thick. You too let Jesus the Lord have your back and not your face. You too beat a retreat.

As for the precise reason why Mark gave up, we are not clearly told what it was. Some have suggested that it was because of his *racial pride and prejudice.*

Or, as others have pointed out, perhaps Mark failed because of *homesickness.*

Or, as some have contended, Mark failed through *fear.*

Whatever the reasons or motives for his retreat, the pitiable fact is that he took the slacker's way out. Some of us have done no better. Before we vent our censure on him, we do well to search our own souls. "Do you know me?" asked a man of a certain noble preacher. The preacher confessed that he did not recognize him. Then quietly, in broken sentences, came the man's confession like some dirge of death. "I used to be a Christian worker," said he, "and influenced thousands to come to Christ. In an unguarded moment I determined to leave my ministry and become rich. My haste for riches was but a snare. I found myself becoming unscrupulous in my business life, and now I am wrecked, certainly for time—Oh, can it be for eternity? I am separated from my wife and my children, whom I shall never see again." As he came to the end of the tragic story, said the preacher, the man rose in any agony and cried out as one rarely hears a man cry, "God have mercy upon me! God have mercy upon me."

The man, like Mark before him, had beat a retreat.

Here was a man who *repented of his failure.* He must have, because, as we shall see in a moment he was finally reinstated in the fellowship of St. Paul and in the work of Christ.

But first take a good look at John Mark as you find him back in Jerusalem. He is home again. A few weeks ago he thought he could never be happy unless he got back to the city and to the comforts of his mother's house. *Is* he happy? Far from it. Here are the old familiar places: the narrow streets, the gleaming white temple, the Tower of Antonio, the Mount of Olives. Yet somehow they have lost their appeal. And here are the old familiar faces: his mother, James the Pastor, and disciples of Jesus who gather weekly for worship and fellowship. Yet strangely they have lost their attraction. What ever is the matter? Is the change in the places and the faces, or is it in the whipped heart of the man who has run away from duty, and from a big job, and from the Lord Christ? Certainly the real change is within himself.

There is the searing shame of being a deserter. There are the haunting regrets of quitting a worthwhile cause. Neither memory nor conscience will let him rest. He thinks—and the Holy Spirit moves within his thoughts. Thinking is dangerous business for anybody who has shied away from what is right. Thinking is frightfully upsetting if you have given a backhanded slap at Jesus Christ. Peter denied Jesus, disowned Him, swore against Him. But we read of Peter that "When he *thought* thereon, he wept." Reflection gave rise to repentance.

A cold rain was beating pitilessly down when a young woman made her way to the pastor's study. The fires of remorse within her could not be quenched by any external flood. "Oh, how could I ever have done it!" was the outburst of her soul, seeking relief in confession. She too was a runaway from duty, a deserter from the camp of God's nobility. The sun of a happy marriage had gone down behind a frowning bank of clouds. Believing herself to be unloved by her husband, she had left both him and the children to live in sin with the son of a well-known citizen. But the romance that promised so much, paid off in bitter coin. The feeling of guilt upon the conscience depressed her. The secrecy surrounding her manner of life was maddening to her. What could she do?

In the quiet of that pastor's office the wisdom of Holy Scripture and the redeeming mercy of Christ were brought to bear upon her wretched case. Mere remorse became true repentance. The sun began to shine once more.

Though there is no reason to believe that John Mark's sin was of that order, something like the young mother's experience of humble penitence came to him one blessed day in far Jerusalem. It is an experience that *must* come to all of us if we are to be healed of our failures.

III

Here was a man who *came back*. First let us make sure of the *fact*, and then we can let our interpretations of it find expression. Two years have passed. Paul and

Barnabas have returned from their first missionary journey. They are ready to go once more. Again the question of a suitable assistant for them comes up for consideration. The record is exceedingly interesting and revealing: "And Barnabas wanted to take with them John called Mark. But Paul thought best not to take with them one who had withdrawn from them in Pamphylia, and had not gone with them to the work" (Acts 15:37, 38).

There had come a day—or probably a night—when he had settled it to confess his desertion and start over again with Christ. It was night, I fancy, when sleep was far from him. He tossed in shame. Where were Paul and Barnabas that night? What hardships might they be suffering for the Master—hardships that he, Mark, should have been sharing and, sharing, should have been relieving? "Christ, forgive me!" The words came achingly from his beaten spirit. "I'll retrace my steps, if only Thou wilt blot out this stain upon my record. Give me Thy strength, Master, and I'll

> Bear the Cross, endure the pain,
> Supported by Thy Word.

And the answer came, like the gliding in of an ineffable calm after the storm has blown itself out. "You have learned your lesson," said the blessed Master. "You have asked for my forgiveness. Would I withold it from you— I who told Peter one day that *he* must be willing to forgive seventy times seven? It is yours, Mark, all yours, this forgiveness of Mine: go in peace, and sin no more."

And the next morning Mark was ready for the open road again. Perhaps Paul was right: Mark may have needed discipline even after renewal. Even so, the fact remains that his comeback was real and glorious. The further fact remains that Paul at last was convinced of the genuineness of the young minister's restoration. To this lovely touch in the New Testament narrative we now turn.

IV

Here was a man who *made good*. More than ten years have gone by since that unhappy day—or night—when Mark, walking out on Paul and Barnabas, retreated to the safety of Jerusalem. Paul is now an old man, frail in health, and a prisoner of Caesar in Rome. He is writing to Timothy, who is at Ephesus. It is Paul's last message before he goes to martyrdom. It is a tender letter. Some of Paul's friends have lately forsaken him: Demas, for example. Others cannot reach him. But Timothy is soon to start for Rome. So Paul writes: "Take Mark, and bring him with thee: for he is very useful in serving me." What a superb tribute to the young man who failed and then made good! No, let us say it differently: what a superb tribute to the healing grace of Christ Jesus the Lord! He can take our failures and turn them into success; He can take our fears and turn them into courage; He can take our prejudices and melt them by His love; He can take us, when we are in full retreat from God and duty, and, laying a rescuing hand upon us, can turn us around to face once more the task that frowned at us and to master the foe that downed us.

If we ask, "Did John Mark really make good?" the answer writes itself in flaming letters across a spacious sky. He became a teacher of Christ in his own right. He served as an evangelist. He was the companion of Peter. He was the comforter of Paul in old age. And, as if that were not enough, he wrote the Gospel by Mark, the first account of the life of Christ ever written —a book that any sane man would rather have written than all the poetry of Tennyson or all the dramas of Shakespeare.

And now, what of ourselves—we who have buckled at the knees when we should have stood up to duty, we with our melancholy retreats from ideal and conviction and task? Are we not haunted by the escapist tricks that we have too often tried? Are we not hurt souls whose pain is all the sharper because we know we have wounded Christ by our falterings and our failures?

Surely there is a bright signal here for us: A man *can* come back! John Mark's case proves it. Christ's cross assures it. His love underlines it. His promise certifies it.

Then let us take our sorry record, bungled and besmirched though it be, and lay it before His eyes. Let's put it under the touch of His hand. Let Him wipe it clean. We shall not be wrong in saying, "Take it, Lord, soiled and smudged as it is, please take it and put it right!"

Then listen, quietly, as He works the miracle of recovery. His whispered assurance will sound something like this: "I will restore to you the years that the locust hath eaten, the cankerworm and the caterpillar . . . and my people shall never be ashamed."

"*I* will restore . . . !"

"*Ye* shall never be ashamed."